MW00910540

SOIL & SPIRIT

SOIL & SPIRIT

Seeds of Purpose,
Nature's Insight & the Deep Work of
TRANSFORMATIONAL CHANGE

IAN C. WILLIAMS

Revive U&i

SOIL & SPIRIT
Seeds of Purpose, Nature's Insight &
the Deep Work of Transformational Change

ISBN	978-1-5445-3812-9	*Hardcover*
	978-1-5445-3813-6	*Paperback*
	978-1-5445-3814-3	*Ebook*
	978-1-5445-3749-8	*Audiobook*

To Trina, for catapulting me into the unknown
and continuing to walk by my side.

CONTENTS

Words so often fall short.

As you read, relax. If fear arises, settle.

When you connect, rejoice.

Purpose and presence go hand in hand.

Let go of striving and remain receptive.

Let compassion, simplicity,
and patience guide you.

All the solutions you seek
begin with sitting still.

AUTHOR'S NOTE

In our ever-increasing technological age, the human being is forced to adapt to and accommodate all sorts of stimuli. Technological advancements evolve at a rate much faster than our biology, leaving our physiology to play a never-ending game of catch-up. Yet life is inherently spiritual, and we have a responsibility to care for ourselves, one another, and the Earth. The contents of this book are intended to be a launchpad for anyone wishing to begin a spiritual life, or for those wishing to deepen their practice. Whether you feel you have not yet begun or are already well on your way, I extend my deepest respect and admiration to you. The objective of this book is to provide you, the modern-day human, with resources to live a more natural and spiritual life.

The spiritual path is ongoing, an ever-evolving voyage through often mysterious and uncharted territories. As much as our egos would like to think otherwise, it is not something we can conquer. As with any journey, there will be milestones along the way. Yet, the great mystery is that this journey has no end. Just as truth is one but goes by many names, the paths toward truth are many—yet they all lead toward a single source: unity.

The words on this page stand out because of the blank space behind them. The paper in this book exists because of the forests now unseen. The sounds you hear come to life in your inner ear. The thoughts that emerge depend on physical synapses and neural circuitry. Dualistic thinking—black or white, all or nothing, bound or unbound—these are paradigms from the past rooted in outdated epistemology. Clinging to them has left us ill-equipped to pursue a path of virtue. The time has come to usher in a new era, one guided by authenticity, curiosity, and collaboration. Cultivating these attributes in ourselves and our societies will lead to *true* spiritual growth.

Ultimately, the unfolding of any path is a process of trans-formation. People often describe it as a process of ascension, though we could just as easily say "descension," return-ing to the core of our being. It is a foundational concept of this book that we are conditioned into the notion of "self." Western colonial thinking—often materialist, reductionist, and individualistic in nature—reinforces this concept. The notion that our lives and bodies are separate from any-thing "other" is embedded in us before we have the cogni-tive ability to consider such a conclusion for ourselves. But does the infant consciously know that she is separate from her mother? Many Eastern and Indigenous spiritual philos-ophies—often more holistic and integrative—speak of a uni-versal oneness. Some suggest that for the soul to touch its purest form, we must disavow the idea of a singular self with clearly defined boundaries separating it from the outside world. If we accept the validity of both viewpoints, where does this leave us? Can we know our place in the world if we do not know ourselves? These questions present challenges to our psyche and identity.

Every challenge, at its core, directly connects to the early acceptance of and belief in our separateness. At the same time, this split also represents a source of infinite opportu-nity. When much of the world chases after Western cultural values of status and wealth driven by the constructs of cap-italism, consumerism, racism, and classism, how do we as a collective orient toward what is and has always been our responsibility: the evolution of humanity? Navigating these dichotomous paradigms may feel like an obstruction to spiri-tual development. However, the paradox reveals a deep truth about humans: we seek to evolve through self-actualization.

So often, words fall short of communicating exactly what we seek to express. In this book, I have taken liberty with the English language. My intention is to bring you to a space *between* the letters, words, and sentences, so that you might interpret the unique message you alone are meant to receive. I hope the words on these pages bring you to a space of inner communion and dialogue. Yes, into a relationship with these concepts—but more importantly, into a deeper relationship with your Self.

Our continuous opportunity to evolve reveals itself in the form of countless challenges—intellectual, interpersonal, and otherwise. Yet those who yearn to grow and pursue a virtuous path can feel the warmth of the sun without obstructive clouds. My deepest desire is that this text will offer what you seek and need most in this time of transformational change.

INTRODUCTION

The word *nature* can be used as a verb, noun, or adjective. To describe one's nature is to describe the fiber of one's being. Yet in our Western conquest of the natural world, we have separated ourselves from nature in all its forms. We extract natural resources in the name of progress and development, without considering the consequences. As a collective, we are at the developmental stage of a toddler, pulling out all the toys for our own amusement and neglecting to put them back.

The term "natural resources" fundamentally defines the natural world as a reservoir to deplete. It also creates the subtle distinction that Mother Nature is separate from us, or that we are somehow separate from her. But Gaia is a living, breathing, emotive being, an intricate and infinite ecosystem capable of deep and intimate communication. When healthy, she speaks in a quiet, subtle manner, through a babbling brook or the coo of a dove. When unhealthy, she speaks in violent fits of "natural disasters," which are becoming increasingly frequent and turbulent. Through climate change, the Earth is reminding us who really has the power.

This book is not an attempt to convince you that climate change is real. The scientific evidence is overwhelmingly clear. In recent decades, we've learned the Earth's ecosystem is more delicate than we ever imagined. Climate collapse is already causing cataclysmic damage and is poised to intensify. Nor is this book meant to shame or guilt you into action. Countless studies reveal these tactics to be ineffective sustainers of change. Yet our collective discord—which includes the state of the climate and public health—screams for change. Deep, purposeful, sustained change.

This book is meant to revive humanity. To restore integrity to the human race, one "individual" at a time. To transform the culture of our civilization by reconnecting us to our true nature—one that coexists with the natural world as natural beings. It is a message that encourages us to embrace the tension of our dichotomous times so that we might rise to the occasion, learn from our challenges, and lean into a cultural paradigm shift that brings about unification.

We often mistake the longing in our hearts as a desire for some *thing*, when in actuality, it is our intuition calling, asking us to contemplate an alternative state of existence. It encourages us to revive our connection to the natural world and restore an eco-reverence that has guided us during every phase of evolution, until now. In essence, intuition asks us to reconnect to Self, spirit, and the soil beneath our feet.

I use the personal language of "you," "me," and "I" because we must always start from where we are. And I use the inclusive language of "we" and "our" because I am right here with you—not separate, advanced, or special in any way, just deeply connected to this path and process. I also speak of self and nonself, because one must come to know self before they can go beyond and access realms of nonself; at least, this has been my experience. A distinction is also made between self and Self. Though not separate entities, the latter is a nod to a higher version of who you already are. The language and concepts in this book may not be your preference, yet I ask you to use them for this exercise in self-exploration. It will be an opportunity to seek and find—or rather uncover and revive—resonance. At times, we will traverse some difficult terrain, both internally and externally.

This book is written and structured from the inside out. We will first explore the inner landscape, the space where every answer exists and every opportunity emerges. We will then move to the social landscape, where one connects to the "outside" world of human beings and how this two-way exchange impacts the wellbeing of life itself. Then we will move to the external landscape, or natural world, the source of all solutions to the challenges we face. Finally, we conclude with the spiritual landscape, a terrain that touches every aspect of our lives.

The spiritual nature of life is woven throughout this text. Spirituality is not a destination, or a thing we do; it is a state of existence. Life is inherently spiritual. One's spiritual process is present in every step and every breath—every encounter and interaction—and often strongest during every episode of discord and discontentedness. The natural model of cross-pollination guides these three main tenets—personal development, ecological reverence, and spiritual evolution—and is critical as we seek to create meaning, purpose, and a better quality of life. This is not a book that will simply suggest you meditate to find bliss. You may have already tried and found it to be quite difficult. Instead, I hope it will serve as a roadmap to get you from where you are to exactly where you are meant to be.

Collectively, we are deep in a phase of evolutionary discord. We have stripped humanity from life and distanced ourselves from the internal processes that have guided us through the millennia, replacing them with consumption and corruption. Yet what is profit without purpose? What is economics without ecosystems? What is evolution without advancement of the soul? Material possessions can never fill the internal void so many of us feel. Consumption will never satisfy the soul's yearning. The soul yearns to be connected, and for that we must acknowledge the interconnected nature of life and love.

The law of interconnectedness makes up the ground on which we stand, in life and in spirit. Our inability to recognize this interconnection to the natural world has brought us here, amidst a crumbling society and ecosystem. If we are to create a life that is not just sustainable but regenerative as well, we must live in unison with ourselves, one another, and the planet.

The body is one singular physiological ecosystem, and so is the Earth. For millions of years, Mother Nature has supported biological evolution, providing more than enough for all who inhabit this planet. She is the Giving Tree, the Tree of Life. Before the human species, no creature had the capacity or the will to exploit the Earth. All animals were able to coexist in a mutually beneficial way, just like the birds and the bees. Then, humans began to pervert this relationship. Without having ever needed to defend herself, the Earth was now startled, bewildered by the toxic abuse she experiences daily. The mistake was ours, believing she was inexhaustible, an endless bounty to extract our desires from. We are simply the byproduct of billions of years of evolution, yet in a matter of centuries, we have brought our species and countless others to the brink of extinction and beyond.

Yet Gaia is always learning, the same way any sentient being does. The long arch of her evolution has seen countless species come and go, though none have met their demise by their own hand. Now, as her delicate ecological balance has been disrupted, she has learned to communicate her frustrations. She bears witness, day in and day out, to the unnecessary and harmful exploitation of her body and breath. Yet, after all this, she continues to provide what is necessary for our survival, remaining benevolent and optimistic. She listens to the sun, and her wind, rain, roots, and soil respond in kind. She sees hope in humanity, despite her frustrations.

The world requires a radical shift. It is unlikely that everyone will take corrective action immediately. However, involving every single person is also unnecessary. We must only reach critical mass. Please help revive what so many of us have lost touch with: eco-reverence. Help strike a balance between doing and nondoing, being and nonbeing, striving and nonstriving. The world needs individuals like you to stand up and carry the torch, to demonstrate there is another way to live. The survival of our species and countless others depends on it.

Please join me on this journey of discovery. It may not be for the faint of heart; however, it contains tools for any person to move into deeper states of awareness. By bridging the gap between nature and spirituality through education and philosophy, we can restore dignity to a species that has become disconnected from a natural way of life. We can facilitate a global movement back to eco-reverence and spiritual integrity. We can acknowledge, accept, and embrace the fact that our sole purpose in life is to uncover our soul's purpose. Together, we can explore soil and spirit.

Always remember: whatever we do not awaken in this lifetime will be waiting for us in the next.

With my deepest sincerity, love, and respect—gassho (a bow of love),

—Ian C. Williams

SECTION ONE

INTERNAL LANDSCAPE

DEFINING THE
INTERNAL LANDSCAPE

The internal landscape encompasses all that is part of our inner domain. It is this internal terrain where we spend every moment of our existence. Of course, our internal landscape does not end where it meets the outer layer of the epidermis, as our thoughts, feelings, and physiology all extend beyond the physical body. Whether we are conscious of these internal processes or not, they govern our lives. When we do not take the time to understand and cultivate them, we become a ship without a rudder. Each of us must dedicate time and energy to exploring the unending landscape that lies within.

Western colonialism suggests that production and consumption will somehow fill our cup. This is the result of materialistic reductionism, which reduces everything to mere matter. If we cannot physically see, dissect, or measure it, then, according to this principle, it must not exist. To follow this logic, one might suppose that if something cannot be produced or consumed, it must not have value.

Science has brought with it many gifts that allow us to understand the world from a truly unique perspective, and there are many parts of our internal landscape that can be physically seen, dissected, and measured. Yet each of us possesses an intuition that senses there is more to life than just physical matter. This sense is part of the internal landscape.

Its essence is ineffable. Yet through awareness and cultivation, it can be made tangible. It can be designed and created, or demolished and destroyed. Just as any physical environment, we have the opportunity to steward and cultivate the landscape within.

A GREATER
CALLING

Globalization suggests the peak of human existence is Western colonialism imposed on the rest of the planet and that its greatest expression is the United States of America. Conveniently written out of the mainstream narrative are the fundamental truths that America was established on stolen land and its infrastructure built on the back of systemic oppression and dispossession. Can something truly be wonderful if it was ethically and morally corrupt from inception? We are called to something greater than this as a species.

Furthermore, the Western constructs of capitalism and consumerism have generated an infinite growth paradigm. This is at odds with the science of materialistic reductionism. How can infinite growth be sustained on a planet that is finite? It must be mentioned that the planet is undoubtedly infinite in her ability to provide for all, so long as we abide by the relationship governing biological evolution: mutuality.

As we begin to unravel the narrative that dominates the West and is accepted by so much of the developing world, we must ask the question: how much longer can this continue? We know the answer. Science tells us we are reaching a point of no return, and our hearts sense this precipice as well. The soul constantly guides us toward a greater calling in response to this crisis. It is this greater calling that has brought this book to your hands, these words to your ears, and this message to your soul. This greater calling that stirs within you precedes your birth and extends beyond your death. It is this greater calling that is now at the forefront of human evolution.

We have an opportunity to realize this calling in our lifetimes. To set the stage so that future generations can elevate humanity to heights unseen. We must learn to define this as our responsibility. This is our greater calling. And though it represents a profound evolutionary step forward, it is also a dutiful journey back to our roots. We are, after all, natural beings—the total sum of cosmic building blocks assembled over endless eons. If we forget our true nature, we separate ourselves from the sustainer of life. But as we remember our true nature, we can answer our calling and navigate this time of transition with dignity.

At this time in evolution, we have more choices than ever before. Why not set the stage to watch the sun rise, rather than watching helplessly as the sun finally sets?

COMING TO TERMS

In order to answer the call, we must come to terms with so much. We must acknowledge from the heights of our institutions down and through the minutiae of our physical bodies that we have strayed from the path and a natural way of life. We must come to terms with the fact that moving humanity forward means taking a step back to regain a wholesome perspective. We must accept that many are living a life that has been bought and sold to them. We must reckon with ourselves and ask the difficult questions about our life, love, and pursuits.

Coming to terms with the natural world means realizing that, without a functional macro-ecosystem, there is no foundation for human life to build upon. As a species that has presumed eminent domain over the planet, we have made ourselves responsible for Earth's ecosystem. Our hubris has led us to believe that the Earth is incapable of providing in abundance for the soon-to-be eight billion people alive on the planet. Our actions reflect that belief, and we have taken matters into our own hands. We have allowed agriculture to become industry. We have allowed drinking water to become industry. We have allowed energy to become industry. The basic needs of human existence are commodities now bought and sold.

It must be emphasized that our current industrial agriculture system disrupts the planet's epidermal layer, the topsoil. By destabilizing the soil, we are taking away one of the most diverse parts of the Earth's ecosystem: trillions upon trillions of bacteria and microorganisms that make up the fungal network and the mycorrhizae that connect plants to the Earth. Think of these like the autonomic processes that your body is dependent upon for survival. The critical symbiotic relation between fungi and the roots of plants is one reason why so many of the solutions to climate change reside within the soil. The Earth's soil is the number one land-based carbon sink available on the planet, and as a dominant species, we possess the capacity to restore it. Through practices such as permaculture, regenerative agriculture, and water stewardship, it is possible to feed the planet and restore the health of Earth's macro-ecosystems.

We must also question our governments and the multinational corporations that buy and sell the Earth and social capital the same way a stockbroker day-trades on Wall Street. Are we to believe these powers have our best interests in mind when their governance favors the industries that contribute to environmental degradation? I am neither condemning them nor condoning them; I am simply calling into question the ethics of their practices. One might argue that civilizations rise and fall over the course of human history and that this is just one more cycle. This may be true, yet have we ever seen the level of globalization that we see today? Have we ever seen the level of influence that multinational corporations have over geopolitical decision-making that we see today? I say this simply to remind you that you are responsible for your own wellbeing and that any form of government or institution should be designed to serve its people. It is meant to encourage within you the agency to live life aligned with the wellbeing of your Self, your community, and the environment.

Those in the global North have become accustomed to the luxury of convenience. But we must also realize that reliable convenience is an unsustainable path for a global civilization. It is a system of greed and corruption, spawned from a deep-seated belief that there is not enough to go around. When we truly sit in the throes of our discomfort, we realize that the hamster wheel of production and consumption is not fulfilling. We feel misalignment between the life we now lead and the opportunity to lead our lives.

Coming to terms may be the most challenging piece of this equation. It feels as though we are letting go of our luxuries and returning to a tribalism that we have evolved beyond. It feels as though we must engage in a process of self-sacrifice. There is no sugarcoating this work, and because of this, some might turn away from it. The question is, are you one of them? I do not believe you are. I believe you are here now because you are following the lead of intuition, seeking deeper meaning and purpose, searching for the experience of being truly alive.

Within this dystopian forecast, I write with unbridled optimism. Because there is good news. We are all addicts—addicted to ideas and ideologies that make up our beliefs. *But addicts can recover!* I am one of them. As with any revolution over the ages, we must reach critical mass. We must also reach a tipping point within ourselves. Coming to terms with the dissonance between our addictive urges and our truth is like peeling a pungent onion. Sometimes the nose runs and the eyes water, yet we persist. We persist because the pain of our self-induced suffering is, at its core, deeply unnecessary and dispensable. We persist because the desire to enjoy the fruits of our labor outweighs the temporary discomfort.

This process of coming to terms represents the first stage of recovery—admitting we have a problem—a process akin to restoring an old vintage mirror. Before taking it down from the attic where it had been forgotten, blowing away the dust, and wiping away the cobwebs, the first order of business is to see its potential. Only then can we embrace the work that lies ahead. The idea, the greater calling, sparks the motivation to reclaim the mirror in the first place. Coming to terms is getting reacquainted with that mirror and orienting oneself to the beauty we can restore, regardless of the hard work required to achieve it.

The process of restoration and revival takes courage and vulnerability. But it also represents an opportunity to come to terms with an unrealized Self—to excavate and redesign our internal landscape. We are willing to face the discrepancy between our actions and our beliefs. We sense that we are here to be of service; we begin to accept that "overtime" may be required to align our purpose with our lived experience. Thus, we muster the courage to polish the mirror, in the hope that we will gain a sense of clarity along the way.

TURNING INWARD

Once we acknowledge a higher purpose and come to terms with what is holding us back, we have begun turning inward, into the garden. This garden is our spiritual home. It is the landscape where self-reflection and development blossom into maturation and self-actualization. For many of us, this garden has not been visited regularly or tended with any conscious intent for quite some time. Parts are filled with cultivars that we have carefully selected. Other parts are overrun due to neglect and inadvertent care. To turn inward is to spend time tending this garden and cultivating the aspects of self that offer meaning, purpose, and clarity in direction.

To do this effectively, and to the depths necessary, we must be willing to spend time alone in this garden. We must bear witness to the neglect that has allowed parts of ourselves to become overgrown or underrepresented. As we begin to recognize these untended aspects of self, we can prune back certain elements to make space for more desirable vegetation.

Sacred texts teach us that we are always divine and benevolent beings, though to truly believe this for ourselves, we may require a sincere process of tending to self.

In the beginning, we must simply commit to facing whatever we discover head-on. This is often uncomfortable, as it requires us to address aspects of self that we have unintentionally neglected or purposefully ignored. This could mean addictive tendencies, codependent relationships, or self-limiting beliefs. Neglecting these pieces of self is a natural part of the human condition. Millions of years of evolution have hardwired us psychologically and physiologically to seek safety and security. However, this has resulted in a human condition that is resistant, if not unwilling, to look at the whole of life.

As we spend time in this garden of self, a fundamental truth reveals itself: *the only way out is in*. Though it may not seem so at times, looking outside is not the way to see inside. The *Tao Te Ching* suggests we do not need to look out the window to see within ourselves. We must pass through the eye of the needle to experience that which our souls desire most. No amount of effort to avoid discomfort will allow us to escape it. No amount of resolve to keep discomfort out will stop it from taking root within. In fact, avoidance and resistance make matters worse. A healthy garden requires time spent managing it before we can obtain a yield. Time to realize that we do not need, nor desire, to be satiated by the external world. It is only that which lies within that can satisfy the soul. This process helps us realize that there is no distinction between internal and external. Torment and anguish are counterweights to joy and pleasure. They are measured on the same scale and part of the same experience. It is these moments of self-relating that teach us how to cultivate a spiritual center.

Turning inward means you have finally come home. Take solace and smile.

SVADHYAYA

Svadhyaya is a term from Hinduism that translates as "self-study," though it can also include study of scripture and the Higher Self. This process of self-study prepares the individual for deeper insight and experiences. By tending to our internal landscape, spending time in the garden of self, we begin to develop greater awareness of Self. Developing this awareness helps us understand the impact particular aspects of our internal landscape have on our development, such as how we respond to certain stimuli, our inner assumptions about the world, the weeds that have taken root in our garden, and, alternatively, the fruits we can cultivate to bring abundance into our lives.

This process is not always pleasant. It can leave us feeling alone, afraid, and bewildered. Reviving an overgrown garden can feel overwhelming at first, like a long, lonely journey with no end in sight. Perhaps that is why many turn away from self-study. The feeling of isolation in a foreign landscape does not call forth respite or relaxation. It may feel foreign because we are not yet literate in the land of the internal and feel ill-equipped to make change. We may long for external guidance but intuitively sense it can only come from within. Though our internal work requires autonomy, we must remember we are always in community. Our sangha—our community—is here to help us forge ahead, providing support to ease the burdens of exhaustion and isolation. And since self-study is essential to our personal and spiritual growth, svadhyaya is equally essential for the growth of the collective.

There are endless self-help gurus promising to guide us toward self-knowing. In the United States alone, self-help is a multibillion-dollar industry, demonstrating that we have a deep desire to know Self. Yet our approach is fundamentally flawed. It is called *self*-help for a reason, and there is deep irony in the notion that we can outsource all our self-care. Indeed, others can provide insight into this process, and attention should be paid to those with such credibility. However, deciphering *exactly* what is needed for our individual growth is ultimately a personal matter. This is why sages and spiritual leaders often answer questions with questions, holding up a mirror so that the inquirer can return to self-contemplation. They encourage the student to look within. After we pull down the mirror of self, svadhyaya removes the sediment that has accumulated on the reflective surfaces until, finally, we can see ourselves clearly.

Individuals who cultivate an inner knowing develop the infrastructure that enables greater societal awareness, and this ability to cultivate awareness through self-study is innate within all of us. We do not need to look outside ourselves to uncover truths that lie dormant within. We must only spend time exploring the inner landscape we have cultivated. Through this process of exploration, we begin to understand the peaks and valleys inside—where life flows naturally and where blockages and fault lines reveal cracks in our foundation.

Svadhyaya is an unending journey of self-discovery. Just as the external landscape changes with the seasons, so too does the internal landscape change with time. With enough awareness, we begin to recognize patterns. These patterns of self provide insight into seeds that were sown long ago. Some of them will need to be uprooted, discarded, and composted. Others will need to be cared for with nurturing intent. Both will fertilize the soil of spirit and enrich the journey that lies ahead.

FIND YOUR
TRUE NORTH

Designing the internal landscape requires that we first understand our inner terrain. Through this process of waking up, coming to terms, and turning inward, we often reorient our internal compass and are redirected toward our true north.

Before we uncover the path to our true north, it helps to have a 360-degree view of self. This full-spectrum awareness allows us to sense the most direct route forward. Science and mathematics tell us the shortest distance from one point to another is a straight line, but anyone who has lived long enough can attest that life rarely unfolds in a linear fashion. Though a direct path may be logical, it is not always possible. This is because we are not alone. We are in relationship with higher powers that guide us toward the experiences we need in order to self-actualize.

By sensing which paths lead toward our greater calling, we can move boldly into the uncharted territories of Self. Our movements are guided by the awareness we have gained through self-study and the feedback we receive from the world around us. We start to balance analytical thought with intuitive reasoning. Thus, the expression of our true purpose becomes a dance—one that allows life to unfold in a natural and winding way while never losing sight of the needle on our compass. Together, orienting to our compass of purpose and responding consciously to life's circumstances, we remain receptive.

As life experiences impact our internal landscape, we must remember our true north is always there to guide us. That is why the discovery of our true north is so important. Sometimes it is obvious because we have been avoiding it or simply never realized it. Other times it requires a deep commitment to self-discovery. Regardless, living life in the direction of our true north moves us closer to our core purpose. Self-study provides insight that awakens our unique genius, the worldly service that only we can offer. As Mark Twain once said, "The two most important days in your life are the day you are born and the day you find out why." Discovering our true north leads us to our core purpose and brings forth a fuller expression of life.

DESIGN YOUR LIFE
IN A DIRECTION

As we declutter the garden of self through the process of self-study, we begin to see our inner topography more clearly. Our natural strengths and weaknesses, affinities and proclivities, beliefs and stories—they all serve as signposts on our journey. They may show us the coping mechanisms we have developed in our attempts to control life. They may point us toward our true north, revealing the attributes of Self that will be essential to our growth. *The way to discernment is through awareness and sensation.*

It is rare for one to sense their true north early on in life. Yet Western culture glorifies this, ultimately perpetuating the hero archetype without providing much support for those of us still learning to read our compass. Until the day we discover our life's core purpose, the best we can do is design our life with direction. For many, the notion that there is a single purpose to life feels limiting or daunting or both. This is an appropriate response! I do not mean to suggest your life exists for only one reason. Rather, I encourage you to consider the *purpose* of your life, and embrace the freedom to express that purpose in an infinite number of ways. We will address ways to develop that awareness beyond a cognitive "knowing." But for now, rest assured that you are supported as you seek truth and justice in all your endeavors.

As we do our best to design our life in a direction, we can feel our true north through sensation. And we can move in that direction with confidence, using intuition. Though an analytical approach can be applied to this process, know that it is also an artform requiring experimentation and redirection. Having not yet identified our core purpose, we *feel* our way through the wilderness of life in search of resonance between body, mind, and spirit.

When designing your life in a direction, synthesize and streamline your awareness through a "life audit." Sit with the specific intention of self-reflection and consider as many aspects of your life as possible. Audit the quality of your relationships, career, vocation, physical health, mental and emotional wellbeing, spiritual connection, dreams, desires, roadblocks— all of it. Get everything out of your head and onto paper so you can begin the sensemaking process with clarity. Let go of the notion that you will figure it all out on your first try. Remember, designing your life in a direction is a process that requires continual engagement to reach its fullest expression.

CONSCIOUS COMMITMENT

Once we have identified a direction, the next step is to make a conscious commitment. You have found your way to this point in life and discovered this book for a particular purpose. As Morpheus says to Neo in *The Matrix*, "I can only show you the door. You are the one that has to walk through it." Having a direction becomes useful only when we hold ourselves accountable and travel toward it. The ongoing process of self-awareness will inform which accountability methods are appropriate for you. Regardless of what those methods are, you must commit to them. Awareness shows you the doorway; conscious commitment allows you to walk through it.

We approach this doorway many times in life and indeed across many lifetimes. Sometimes we are consciously aware of these moments, and other times we are not. Conscious commitment is the tether that anchors you to the courage necessary for self-actualization. It enables you to decipher the meaning of your experiences and answer your greater calling. Without conscious commitment, we become a balloon that has broken free from a child's hand, lost to the whims of the wind and drifting aimlessly through the vast expanse of open space that is life itself.

Make this commitment to your greater calling here and now. Live purposefully as you find meaning along the path of your true north. Perhaps it begins with daily affirmations, or writing a personal memorandum of understanding. Perhaps you will perform a ceremony or ritual to demonstrate your commitment. Whatever you do, do it sincerely and with integrity. Hold yourself accountable in ways that go beyond the most basic levels of behavior modification. You have the opportunity and responsibility to wake up, get out of bed, and begin anew.

You are here for a reason. We are all here at a pivotal time in the existence of our species. It is our generation's greatest calling to take responsibility for ourselves, one another, and the natural world. Paradigms of the past have brought us to the brink of extinction. The revolution of the individual requires us all to move beyond the bureaucracy of institutions, benevolent as they may be, and embrace a natural life. The Earth is no longer asking this of us; she is demanding it. It is our choice whether we will commit to answer her call.

INTERNAL
EDGE ZONES

An edge zone is where two parent ecosystems come together. The area where they meet is more productive and fertile than either of the parent ecosystems individually. You may be familiar with the common saying "there is no growth in the comfort zone and no comfort in the growth zone." While growth can bring discomfort at first, one can become comfortable with the process of growth, especially in the edge zones where exponential growth is possible.

An infant studies her mother's every movement and the sound of her voice, and a healthy mother reciprocates the child's love and attention. The space between the infant and the mother is an edge zone, where thought and emotion meet. Within a space like this, we can observe interactions among thoughts, emotions, and beliefs. How our physical and energetic bodies interact represents another edge zone, and while we might observe one more easily than the other, both are essential. It is our calling to explore these spaces with the same nurturing intent as a mother with her child.

Millions of years of evolution have made the human brain capable of intricate assessments and computations. But the brain has not yet learned to make a firm distinction between internal emotional vulnerability and external, life-threatening circumstances. Each induces fear and triggers similar neurological responses. If exploring our internal landscape incites fear, we must remember that we possess the ability to regulate our physiological responses and transform them into something greater. By intentionally exploring our edge zones, we can retrain our fear responses through regular exposure.

Internal edge zones are numerous, as there are an infinite number of ecosystems within. They include states of intellect, emotion, energy, biology, and more. In the process of self-actualization, it is our responsibility to seek out the spaces where these states interact, to become an internal explorer committed to the process of self-actualization. Recall the wise leaders of Indigenous cultures who have long understood we are in relationship with our surroundings. Our internal landscape is not a terrain to be conquered—it is an ecosystem to be explored with compassion, curiosity, and courage.

AWAKEN YOUR LIFE'S
CORE PURPOSE

Whether or not you believe in fate, your life has a core purpose, waiting to be awakened. Some say that "everything happens for a reason" to excuse themselves from personal responsibility. Indeed, there is reason in everything. Sometimes those reasons are obvious, and other times a substantial amount of reflection is required to uncover them. Regardless, *our sole purpose in life is to discover our soul's purpose.* Your unique traits and talents, coupled with your life experiences, create the circumstances you need to continue your soul's evolutionary process.

We need not believe in God to integrate this concept into our lives. Instead, it may be helpful to think of our life's core purpose more broadly as the convergence of fate and free will. Fate is typically understood as the life events we do not have control over, while free will encompasses all that is influenced by our personal choice. The intersection where these two domains come together is an edge zone that is abundantly fertile. We must learn to strike a balance and allow fate and free will to exist in a mutually beneficial way. As we consciously commit to exploring these spaces, we can also turn to leaders who help us cultivate the balance we seek. The more adept we become at exploring our internal landscape, the better equipped we are to assist others in their own explorations.

Awakening our life's core purpose requires an internal fortitude that few choose to invoke. Many of us find ourselves leading a life and lifestyle that has been handed down by others. For those of us committed to seeking God (or finding a balance between fate and free will), we must release the notion that success means safety, security, and the luxury of convenience. We must move beyond our basic needs and learn to manage our desires. It is for this reason that self-sufficiency is paramount. By meeting our own needs and regulating our own desires we become self-sufficient. We are then free to pursue a more meaningful life. But natural laws apply to a natural life. Just as diversity creates resilience in nature, self-sufficiency need not equal isolation. Everything exists in relation to everything else.

Being "awake" can have many definitions. Here, it means walking your path as a truth seeker and actualizing your spiritual purpose. For if you are not living your truth, are you truly living? If you do not water your garden, will it ever grow? Will everything need to shift, or very little? It depends on how far you have strayed from your own true north. Inhabit and sense the space of living out your core purpose: what do you notice or feel? Remember the depth of this process. Defining the work as "hard" represents only one layer of understanding. Being aligned with our core purpose creates a magnetic draw that pulls us closer to our frequency of destiny. Always remember that you do not walk this path alone. Others will offer guidance and support, and you will do the same for them.

Living your life's core purpose requires a certain "whatever it takes" mentality. These shifts may be challenging. In fact, they *should* be challenging. The soul craves a good challenge, and it is wise to remember that the changes you make will lead to a greater calling and purpose. There is nothing more rewarding than living through that purpose. Eventually, you will feel as though there is no other way you could possibly live your life. As you seek the truth of your virtuous path, you will find your home inside your Self. You will become the leader who shines light on dark spaces.

MINDFULNESS

Mindfulness is often associated with a child-like presence for good reason. Until now, we have largely explored the steps required to reorient one toward their true north. For most, this will require a fair amount of heavy lifting and emotional labor. Certain aspects of life will no longer feel right, and we will have to distance ourselves from them or discard them entirely. Other aspects of life will call us to lean in and explore, searching for a feeling of resonance. The child naturally lives in this state of exploration and curiosity.

Here, resonance means aligning our actions with our greater calling. Using our ability to sense alignment, we can recognize when we are in or out of harmony. Harmony means alignment—physically, mentally, emotionally, and energetically—with our frequency of destiny. Popular culture teaches The Law of Attraction and manifestation with an outside-in approach. In other words, what can the world bring me? However, the universal balance means there is also a corresponding inside-out approach. What can you bring to the world? Resonance is being aligned with both inside-out and outside-in so that we may harmonize with the frequency that guides our higher purpose.

As children individuate and pass through different stages of development, we see them ebb and flow, moving in and out of harmony. As adults, we engage in that same process, falling in and out of resonance. "Falling out" means we have forgotten that the universe guides us in every moment. "Falling in" means we are aligned, committed, and centered on the path toward awakening our life's core purpose. *The process of feeling for, finding, and harmonizing with resonance is mindfulness embodied.* Embodying a benevolent child-like presence helps us stay connected to guidance from powers beyond our comprehension.

Mindfulness can serve an infinite number of purposes. We use it as a tether to anchor us to the present moment. We use it as a scalpel to dissect the situation at hand. We use it as a surveyor's map to maintain a higher perspective so that we never mistake the forest for the trees. Mindfulness guides us toward the parts of our internal landscape we are called to explore. It is the air we breathe, the sky we see, and the waters we sail upon. Though mindfulness can be applied in an infinite number of ways, there are objective principles that govern its cultivation. We can think of mindfulness as the convergence of breath, body, and brain—a single shared language that emerges if one commits to cultivating their inner knowing.

There are no words that can truly describe the nature of mindfulness. The more we attempt to explain it through language, the further we get from truly knowing its nature. Labeling the world around us transforms our experiences into concepts that only have meaning through the context of our thoughts. Mindfulness conveys a more subtle, universal truth. It connects us to the core of other beings while maintaining a connection to our own. It encourages us to consider the compulsions of body and mind, and it calms the waters of lust and dampens the fires of desire. Every moment is a gift from Creator, providing us another opportunity to be present. When we truly sit in the present moment, we discover that there are no thoughts to think, only an experience to be had. Mindfulness is the key that turns the lock of perspective.

Over the millennia, mindfulness has shaped a secure and steady path to greater awareness. Practices such as yoga, qigong, taiji, meditation, martial arts, and many others all share the same language at their core. It is the language of body consciousness. Concepts such as "gut instincts" or an "inner knowing" are the result of our ancestors cultivating awareness through the art of mindfulness. This intelligence remains stitched into our karmic DNA. You have undoubtedly experienced this before. Consider the subtle thought to grab that seemingly irrelevant item before walking out the door that you dismiss in the moment, only to discover later in the day it would have proved useful. Or a spur-of-the-moment decision to take a different route home from work, only to learn your traditional route was closed due to construction. Or the unprompted memory of a loved one and a feeling of their presence, only to discover later they recently passed on. Writing off these synchronicities as chance occurrences denies our own inner wisdom.

Mindfulness means noticing the subtle cues our body provides. It is the loving partner of intuition that allows us to decipher friend from foe, fact from fiction, and false alarm from a firm sense of self. It is the knife that cuts the bread of awareness. However, before we can receive its messages, we must understand and believe our body is sentient. The body is always talking, and it offers us the ever-present opportunity to perceive the world through more than cognitive intellect. True consciousness requires a balanced understanding of the breath, body, and brain. Every human shares the same biological functions that can be used to communicate with the greater beyond. The truly attuned mindfulness practitioner understands there is no such thing as separateness. Mindfulness allows us to perceive the true nature of the entire cosmos and its universal language: consciousness. Mindfulness generates clarity that allows us to connect to our life's core purpose in the present moment.

ENERGY ARTS

If awareness and mindfulness are partners, then intuition is the offspring. Intuition is not some esoteric knowledge reserved for only a few; it is buried deep within all of us, threaded to the core of our being. Humans have used energy arts to cultivate awareness for thousands of years. *The most direct path to intuition is the art of connecting body with breath and paying attention to what emerges.* Intuition is a seed that lies dormant until the conditions are ripe for germination. It is our responsibility to create those conditions in our garden and bring intuition forth from the confused cauldron of the monkey mind and undisciplined heart.

Deep within us, there is a solid foundation waiting to be uncovered. The energy arts of yoga, qigong, taiji, meditation, martial arts, and others provide the structure for us to safely navigate the descent into stillness where intuition resides. These practices simplify the process of developing a relation-ship between our breath, body, mind, and spirit. They are technologies that can be used to help us consistently return to a space of inner knowing. There is deep purpose in the sacred practice of these art forms, and many are staples in monastic life for good reason. They provide the foundation of self-regulation required to awaken our life's core purpose. Therefore, we should approach them with reverence.

Energy arts connect us to our core so that we might live from our spiritual center. This is one reason they are often described as "practices" intended for self-cultivation. They are proven methods to support spiritual growth and development. The practitioner creates conditions to consciously commune with a Higher Self and come to know the subtleties of life, such as the difference between meditating and being meditative. Energy arts guide our existence by teaching us how to *be* through conscious exploration of what we *do*.

We should pay attention to how we study these practices and with whom. Just as poor instruction in mathematics will lead to the incorrect application of formulas, so too will poor instruction in the energy arts lead to incorrect application of such methods. Observe the sensations you experience in every aspect of your practice. Ask yourself: Does the instructor embody authenticity and integrity? Does the energy art itself speak to you? Does it provide the mental, emotional, and physical conditioning that *you* require? Does the practice simplify the process of awakening, or does it complicate it? These are all questions to consider as you travel along your path toward deeper meaning and purpose. Listen for guidance from within and trust your own instincts as you develop greater awareness.

TOOLS IN YOUR
TOOL BELT

Use the breath to connect the mind to sensations of the body. After all, it is our body that receives and processes stimuli from our surroundings; the mind only interprets. Relying on the mind to stay fully present is a mistake, as this is not the nature of the mind itself. As we continue to polish the mirror of self and look inward, we can use the breath as a means of stabilizing our awareness. Focusing our awareness on the breath connects us to the messages of the body. The breath holds our attention and engages us in a meditative state. It enables us to face discomfort head-on, breathing our way through the fear response.

The breath is one tool for self-cultivation that all humans possess, yet it is only a single tool in our tool belt. Each individual is unique, with their own distinct purpose. Naturally, different tools will serve different individuals. Some may access intuition through the energy arts, others may find their way in through other avenues. As we cultivate self-awareness and begin to understand the nature of mindfulness, we develop from novice to apprentice to journeyperson. With patience and persistence, we become the master craftsperson of our internal landscape. Through breadth and depth of experience, we never encounter a circumstance where we cannot adapt a tool in our tool belt to meet the needs at hand.

However, the tools in our tool belt today may not serve us tomorrow; the job site is always changing. As life shifts, we must respond accordingly. In the beginning, we tend to carry as many tools as possible so that we never encounter a challenge we are unprepared for. Eventually, we recognize we are carrying too much weight and choose to discard tools that no longer serve us.

Commit consciously to this process of analysis and remain receptive to the feedback you receive. What you think you need may not be necessary, and what you deem irrelevant may be essential to your development.

Only to the untrained eye does nature appear as a static system. A mindful observer will notice the subtle shifts that occur from moment to moment. This awareness reveals an essential truth about life itself: *change is the only constant.* Therefore, we must learn to approach life as travelers and

**Consider the tools in your
current tool belt.**

- What coping mechanisms have you
  developed that are now a crutch?

- What will it take to release them?

- What skills or talents have you
  long desired to develop but never
  taken the time to acquire?

- What would it take to obtain them?

teachers. Every empire built over the course of human history has been lost to the sands of time. The traveler reserves the right to move toward new discoveries as curiosity guides them. The teacher understands when it is time to become a student again. Do not fall victim to the belief that life's circumstances will settle. Instead, calm the waters *inside*. Embrace shifts as they arise—and watch them pass just as the sunflower follows the sun across the sky.

THE FIVE A'S

Aside from death, change is one of the few experiences guaranteed in life. These transitions can be instantaneous and acute or seismic and prolonged. At times, it will be difficult to move away from our comfort zone and the life we have grown accustomed to. But it can also bring balance, as we sense alignment with our life's core purpose. Growth requires change, and it may feel as though we are drifting further from those we love. Coincidentally, we begin to know others more intimately as we deepen our understanding of Self. Just as it is difficult to perceive the tectonic plates shifting beneath our feet, it can also be difficult to sense the subtle changes in life. Yet we know that they are always there. For those of us embarking on the journey of awakening our life's core purpose, change will be a familiar constant.

This process of change often occurs in a cyclical manner. First, we must *acknowledge* that change is required and *accept* that it is coming. Afterward, we can make *accommodations* to create space for the change. Finally, we *adapt* and learn to embrace what is new. As we move through these phases it is essential that we do so with *authenticity*, or we have missed an opportunity to cultivate a sustainable, balanced internal landscape. The Five A's—acknowledge, accept, accommodate, adapt, and authenticity—illustrate the constant growth cycle that orients us toward our true north.

Acknowledgment is simply the first moment of awareness, and it comes in many forms. It often begins subconsciously as a natural response to discord. When the Earth senses a shift is needed, she acknowledges through sensation, such as when a natural spring emerges from the ground to create a stream. Of course, this water comes from somewhere such as an underground aquifer. It is the same for us as humans: our underground aquifers are reservoirs of energy that often flow unconsciously. Sometimes we call forth that energy with intention, and other times it springs forth naturally. Regardless, acknowledgment gives the impending change traction as it moves up from our subconscious mind. Once we perceive the change consciously, we often begin to play games with ourselves. Some of us respond too hastily while others prolong the process unnecessarily. Either way, whether or not we desire it, change has begun as soon as acknowledgment occurs.

Once a natural spring emerges, it does not follow a predetermined path. Instead, it follows the path of least resistance. The same can be said for our process of change. As energy springs forth, we allow it to travel the path of least resistance by *following it with our awareness rather than guiding it with our intention.* Eventually, enough energy gathers that it will carve out the riverbed of change.

Once we have acknowledged the change, acceptance is ahead. By now, the subconscious mind has already integrated the impending change, making it our responsibility to mirror that acceptance in our conscious Self. This marks a tipping point. Until now, the waters of change have been flowing down the river of life. Acceptance is the moment just before the river reaches the waterfall. When done healthily, acceptance is a smooth transition. When we struggle, our energy becomes agitated and the waters begin to churn. As we prepare to crest the falls, conscious commitment supports us in the moment.

As with any skill, acceptance becomes easier with practice. Due to the nature of free will, humans can choose to change or not. Certain communities suggest that change happens when the pain of life is greater than the fear of change itself. Our conditioning suggests that if change requires risk, we should postpone it until we feel prepared or avoid it altogether. Yet to lead a spiritual life, we must recognize there is always risk when awakening our life's core purpose. That purpose draws us to our life's core the same as a honey bee is drawn to the center of a flower. We are compelled to act.

Accommodation comes next. This is the moment in time when the river reaches the top of the waterfall. When change is forced upon us we must accept reality as it is. In those cases, accommodation is made in response to an external event, as with the unexpected loss of a loved one. Other times, change happens internally, such as when we identify a desire and orient our actions accordingly. Ultimately, we must make accommodations for change both internally and externally. This can require a great deal of emotional labor. But once we accept that change is constant, we hold space for it in our lives. For growth to occur, decay is often required. Like a river rock, our surfaces will be smoothed by the waters of change as we begin to accommodate the ebb and flow of life.

Finally, we reach adaptation. At this point, the water crests the falls and we find ourselves in freefall. We have accepted the change and are making the modifications required for growth. We must adapt in order for life to be sustainable. It is this process of adaptation that allows any being to reach equilibrium with its surroundings. The beauty of this process is evident in nature. When a wildfire ravages a forest, the forest floor enters a period of rapid regeneration to protect the bare soil. When a tree falls from the riverbanks, the water flows over, around, and underneath the obstruction. In time, the tree will be carried away and the river will adapt once again. Though constant adaptation occurs, balance is always present. Not surprisingly, human wellbeing requires growth and change, undertaken with a balanced approach. This is the process of evolution itself.

The Five A's are a rather technical description of change. The preceding paragraphs contain no real instruction on navigating the emotional peaks and valleys of such a process. Truthfully, there simply is no elegant answer. The conviction of conscious commitment, mindfulness, and the tools in your tool belt are all that is required to navigate these waters—and, of course, faith itself. This is the function of authenticity. Only you can determine whether you will engage in this process authentically. You are making this change to navigate your own river and awaken your own life's core purpose. Embrace the freedom to live fully and wholeheartedly without reasons or justifications. Emotional turmoil is guaranteed, but always remember that the work itself is more important than the fear of change. As the Buddha teaches, *pain is inevitable, but suffering is optional.*

Often, the change itself is less important than *how* it is generated. Mindful change informs our self-development process and shows us the path of least resistance. Living life in the direction of your true north requires integrity. Without this, our spiritual house is built on top of quicksand. We leave ourselves nothing solid to anchor into when the waters of life become turbulent and the Earth shifts beneath us. If you have not already, make an agreement with yourself here and now to engage in this process authentically. At the end of the day, you lay your head down on your own pillow. You know what authenticity and integrity feel like. What will empower you to live an authentic life? Reflect on this deeply, because when you know the answer, nothing will draw you away from the magnetic pull of your true north.

THE
PHYSICAL BODY

Our exploration of the internal landscape would be entirely incomplete without mention of the physical body. Consciousness is perhaps the most recent by-product of human evolution. The brain evolved within the body that houses the soul. Even for those who do not believe in the soul, the physical body contains all the essential elements of life. Countless physiological processes operate in unison to create a singular experience of life. And we possess the ability to influence and enhance that physiology. If we do not take care of the physical body, we miss the opportunity to liberate our soul. When we choose to care for ourselves, we enhance the experience of life itself. In the same way that the sun at dawn awakens the world around us, understanding the physical nature of our existence shines light on the topography of our internal landscape.

Science tells us the body is made up of mostly empty space. The atoms and molecules are a symphony of movement expressed at the cellular level, and this dance forms the building blocks of our vital organs and tissues. Combined, we see multiple systems emerge and operate in unison to create what we perceive as a singular organism. Nature is built the same way, and we are natural beings.

Bacteria, microorganisms, and fungi exist within the soil, the plant kingdom is dependent upon the health of that soil, and animals are dependent upon the health of the plants. While Western science often sees the world as an infinite series of singularities, each of these elements form systems that contribute to a greater ecosystem. It is the interaction of those systems that create wonder and awe. The curl of the caterpillar as it crawls along a leaf, the quieting of nature as a storm cell rolls in, or the appreciation of a panoramic landscape from a vista. The same reverence can be directed toward the physical body as we learn to appreciate our own internal landscape and ornate interdependence.

We must see ourselves as intricately connected once again. We may perceive separation between what is underneath and outside the epidermal layer the same way we might perceive a barrier between what is below and above ground. Yet we are exchanging particles with the world around us all the time and water, as well as carbon, is cycling from sky to ground and back again. Are the boundaries we perceive really as definitive as we believe? To conclude that our physical body exists simply to support the six inches between our ears where we think consciousness resides is to deny billions of years of intelligent evolution. A healthy physical vessel is the foundation—the soil—of a healthy internal landscape.

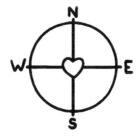

THE FOUR
BUILDING BLOCKS OF
PHYSICAL HEALTH

When we truly observe an organism or ecosystem, it is clear that a great number of inputs produce what we perceive as a single output. As we integrate this awareness, the interdependent nature of life becomes undeniable. This awareness represents a threshold of transition in our perceptive abilities. We begin to see the world for what it truly is. Interdependence becomes our default paradigm, and we relate naturally with the surrounding landscapes. When this awareness is applied to our physical body, it elevates our health and wellbeing substantially.

Nutrition, energy, strength, and flexibility are the building blocks of physical health, and nutrition is the first cornerstone. The food we eat and the liquids we drink provide nutrients at the cellular level, but more than that, the act of eating is a sacred moment of connection. Nutrition is an opportunity to commune with the natural world every time we sit down to eat. Just like fixing our gaze on a fire at night, the act of sharing a meal is woven into our evolutionary DNA.

It is not coincidental that the rise of the industrial food system has correlated with the rise of chronic disease. There is not a single diet that is best for all people, because as a species, we evolved on different parts of the Earth, and this impacted our various food preferences. Still, consideration must be paid to the ecological sustainability of our various diets. Ultimately, we find that appropriate consumption and responsible management of food systems create a natural symbiosis between people and the planet. Michael Pollan's famous line is a good rule of thumb: "Eat food, not too much, mostly plants." Integrate awareness into your relationship with nutrition. A conscious commitment to eat healthily and mindfully will wash away the vast majority of your physical and emotional impediments.

Nutrition generates a great deal of our energy. While making the distinction between energy and Qi (chi) would be too detailed for the purposes of this book, know at least that your energy levels and physical health are closely correlated to the amount and quality of your Qi. Turn to Taoist texts for a more comprehensive overview. In short, Qi is bioelectromagnetic energy that permeates everything and can be cultivated in a great number of ways. Pure natural environments contain a great deal of Qi. This, and the negative ions inherent in these spaces, account for much of their restorative capacities. Generally speaking, the wilder a place is, the more energy it has. Thus, it is essential for the health of all beings on Earth that we re-wild the planet.

Energy can also be influenced by emotion. You may notice that after a "negative" interaction with another human, your energy levels drop. Conversely, a "positive" experience may cause your energy levels to rise. Due to the nature of emotion, the energy derived from these interactions is fleeting and should not be counted on for wellbeing. It is best to take a steady approach to energy through the cultivation of Qi. This is another area where energy arts prove essential to health and wellbeing. Managing your energy is critical as you seek to sustain the awakening of your life's core purpose. Consider your energy frequently and manage it wisely.

Functional strength is also imperative to good health. Qi flows through primary channels in the body, which can be thought of as an energetic circulatory system (Ayurveda refers to these channels as *nadis*, traditional Chinese medicine refers to them as *meridians*). When the body becomes stiff or rigid through a lack of full spectrum movement, environmental conditions, or mental and emotional impediments, it becomes difficult for energy to flow freely. If we think of Qi as bioelectromagnetic energy, the body is essentially a battery that circulates a charge. When the muscle tissues are tight and toned the energy moves more efficiently and the body has a greater carrying capacity.

Functional strength is imperative for proper Qi flow, and both are essential for longevity. Strength serves as the bridge between function and mobility. The goal is to pursue fitness for functionality, not vanity. An overly aggressive fitness regimen is not required. Instead, remember that consistency is key. Pay specific attention to the core as it houses all the vital organs. Static strengtheners such as plank pose or horse stance are great for all-around conditioning. Through awareness and reflection, design a fitness routine that addresses your specific needs and serves the body as a whole.

Flexibility is the final building block, because it is the bridge between the physical body and the natural rhythm of life. While nutrition, energy, and strength are all essential to good health, *flexibility teaches us that true strength requires yielding in all areas of life.* It is essential for mobility and will keep us agile in our later years. When paired with body awareness, flexibility will always overcome brute force. The same can be observed in nature. As the river flows through the rock basin, the flexibility of the water carves away the

brute strength of stone. Ultimately, we can see this principle arise everywhere, as when the pioneering species arrive
quickly after the forest fire.

Remember to consider flexibility within the context of a
functioning whole. Muscle tissue, fascia, tendons, and liga-
ments are all connected underneath the epidermis, anchored
to a skeletal structure that may be out of alignment after
years of neglect. Holistic movement practices such as qigong,
taiji, and yoga asana are best suited for true strength and
flexibility. Learn the intricacies of your physical body and
discover where you are storing stagnant energy. From there,
leverage the tools in your tool belt to release those blockages
and create space for your life's core purpose.

These four building blocks of physical health form the
foundation for psychological and spiritual wellbeing. Our
brain and spirit are anchored in the body, though they are
not bound by it. A deep understanding of our physical nature
allows us to transcend it. We can deepen our awareness of
the cosmos by deepening our awareness of Self. The same
way an infant learns through observing the physical environment, we can learn about universal reality through exploration of our physicality.

SELF-REFLECTION

Self-reflection represents the next layer of health and well-being. From the most basic to the extremely advanced, self-reflection is the Gemini twin of awareness. Grounding self-reflection in application makes awareness more tangible. As we consider illustrations of this truth in a moment, remember that self-reflection is unique to every individual. Indeed, there are countless teachers and ideologies who can aid in our exploration. But ultimately, it is our responsibility to translate these lessons into a language that fits our internal landscape.

Consider self-reflection in physical form. If body awareness reveals a tight hamstring muscle, self-reflection suggests what to do about it: stretching. This is the first phase of self-reflection; the next phase occurs when we apply that awareness and stretch our hamstring. Developing disciplines around nutrition follows the same principles. Many who eat food from the industrial agriculture food system are riddled with dietary sensitivities. Basic laws of nature apply. If the plants and animals we ingest experienced suboptimal health, we inherit their dis-ease. Yet if this is the only food we have ever eaten, then the physical body knows nothing else. When we apply awareness to our eating, we may notice our energy levels drop after a meal, our mood changes, or we begin to clear our throat. In this example, self-reflection would be taking the time to consider the food consumed, devising a plan to identify the culprits, and taking action to eliminate them from our diet.

Inconsistencies in the physical body manifest as irregularities in mood and mindset. Early on in spiritual development, outside stimuli heavily influence our mental and emotional state. By their very nature, emotions flit about like a butterfly moving from flower to flower, and the mind swings back and forth like a monkey in a tree. We struggle to reconcile the soul's search for steady growth with the habits we inherit from our social conditioning. However, it is possible to systemize our mental and emotional wellbeing through proper movement, nutrition, and other practices. A well-regulated mind serves as ballast to stabilize our emotional whims, and this alone will do a great deal to regulate our mood.

Although we are unable to control our surroundings, many of us attempt to do so time and again. Instead, we could, and indeed should, turn our energies inward. While we can optimize physical health through systemization, we can also regulate mental and emotional wellbeing through acceptance and self-reflection. As we study our mind, mood, and messages from the body, a detailed picture of our internal landscape emerges. This picture reveals proclivities, presumptions, perspectives, and much more. This process of self-reflection and applied awareness allows us to access self-regulation. For it is only when we understand these aspects of ourselves and where they take root within us that we can begin to let them go.

The same process applies to one's spiritual path. As we become fluent in the skill of identifying aspects of Self, we understand the composition of our internal landscape. This awareness points us toward the lessons we are meant to learn. These lessons could include releasing our expectations of another to be free from their influence—or identifying our self-limiting beliefs to enhance our sense of self-worth. Perhaps they include acknowledging our passions to connect our profession to our vocation. Ultimately, applying self-reflection moves us closer to our true north as we endeavor to awaken our life's core purpose.

Self-reflection is an essential tool in everyone's tool belt. Though it looks different for everyone, it brings us to the same space—a place where our awareness allows us to engage the meta-ability to see stimuli for what it is, how it is influencing us, and what the most appropriate response might be.

One final note about self-reflection: there is a chasm of difference between reaction and response. Reacting is knee-jerk, involuntary, and without conscious awareness. Responding is a methodical approach to life and governs the way we move through the world. During earlier stages of self-development, reaction may be all we have. Leftover from a time in life when the ability to respond was lacking, the skill was not modeled, and the prefrontal cortex was underdeveloped. As we travel deeper in self-actualization, we become more stable through responsiveness. Balance is expressed in the physical, mental, emotional, and spiritual bodies as we continually refine our ability to respond. Just as a tree finds strength and stability from roots unseen, we find strength and stability that reside at the core of our internal landscape.

BODY
CONSCIOUSNESS

Meditation is the language of the body. Many of us could stand to become more fluent in this language and broaden our understanding of it. Indeed, the monk meditates on his sitting cushion, the yogi meditates in movement on her mat, the endurance athlete finds a meditative state on the trail, and the teacher enters a flow state while educating their students. Formal meditation is simply a tool that allows one to access body consciousness. It is a training ground that offers a doorway to wisdom. Wisdom resides where experience meets intellect. In other words, wisdom resides in the body. This is why intuition is often associated with a gut feeling. Developing awareness through meditation leads us to the understanding that body consciousness is the ultimate instructor.

As we develop an intimate understanding of our internal landscape, we enhance our awareness of Self. Consider your body a sentient and spiritual being. This awareness encourages us to listen to our own higher consciousness rather than seeking guidance from others who are equally confused. In moments of peak awareness, body consciousness grounds our insight in a physical form. The runner finds their perfect stride on the trail, the basketball player finds their perfect shooting form, or the martial artist responds intuitively with the perfect technique. At our core, we are all connected to body consciousness. It is the physical awareness that buttresses our attempts to live mindfully.

Remember, the body is coded with a universal wisdom refined over time. It is an antenna, tuning fork, and stereo speaker all in one—a nuanced communication device capable of receiving and transmitting an infinite number of messages. Thus, we require a calm mind and a composed heart to decipher its code. Through conscious commitment and repetition, we can develop the ability to decipher the body's messages. We cannot *will* ourselves to hear the messages of the body; we must *allow* ourselves to listen as the body speaks. The more we do this, the more we develop our perceptive abilities. Listening to the body is like listening to multiple radio stations simultaneously through a single receiver.

It may sound challenging, and it can be, but we are always processing multiple frequencies at once. By embracing the art of body consciousness, we can learn to be literate in the language of the soul.

MANAGE
YOURSELF

As we delve deeper into the internal landscape, we can see that navigating it requires us to enter uncharted territories. If we get lost in the forest and lose our way, we may never make it through to see the wondrous clearing on the other side. This means our journey also requires the ability to manage ourselves. Self-management is the art of infusing mindfulness into our daily actions in a disciplined way.

Distraction is not inherently negative, but we must learn to decipher intentional avoidance from earnest efforts to cultivate the Self. Again, there are scientific principles that can keep us oriented toward our true north, but this discerning process within us is more of an art form. If we distill it to its scientific principles alone, we strip away the heart and the mysticism.

When we infuse our lives with a higher perspective, we not only see the forest for the trees—we soar above the forest altogether. The eagle does not lose her way, no matter how far she travels. Her vision is clear and her purpose is direct. This is our opportunity, as well. Through the process of self-management, we can trim away the excess and remain connected to what matters most. This makes self-regulation a part of awakening. If we are not yet aware of our core purpose, how will we discover it? Once we are aware of our core purpose, how will we actualize it? The oak tree understands intuitively that to reach higher it must root deeper. More nutrients from the soil will sustain its growth, and more stability in its root structure will keep it upright. We must manage our own resources for continual growth and development.

Self-management is not something that prevents us from living our fullest life—it is precisely what enables us to live life fully. We have been taught that freedom means the ability to fulfill every desire, when, in actuality, true freedom is being free from desire and from the habits that keep us trapped within the confines of our beliefs. To answer our greatest calling, we must dive deep into the soil of Self and realize that everything necessary to awaken our core purpose is already within us.

EDUCATE, MODIFY, IMPLEMENT

Not every action needs to be premeditated, though it should be done with mindful intent. The fledgling mind prefers to think of life in a linear fashion, the same way that we perceive time, while a developed mind recognizes the natural shape of progress to be cyclical. This is not to suggest that we are stuck traveling in circles. Rather, the path of spiritual development is more like a helix, shaped by the natural laws of the universe. When we stop perceiving our lives in a linear way, we find prosperity is in continuous motion.

Regardless of how our internal landscape unfolds, we must remain engaged in the *process*. To awaken our life's core purpose is to embark on a journey of self-refinement. In this process of refinement, we *educate* ourselves, *modify* our behavior, and *implement* new lifestyle choices that reflect our newfound awareness. The *educate, modify, implement* feedback loop represents a cyclical process that can be used to structure our self-reflection and spiritual development.

Education should not be associated with mere intellectual development. The world will always present an endless stream of stimuli, and many of these offer a sort of artificial womb, a place to feel as though we are developing ourselves, when in actuality, we are distracting ourselves. Self-accountability is an essential ingredient to personal growth and development. To educate ourselves means quite simply to enhance our awareness and expand our horizons. The more honest we are with ourselves, the more accurate our understanding of Self becomes. The more awareness we practice, the less we need protection. The need for self-preservation dissipates because we no longer see ourselves as separate from the outside world.

Knowledge becomes wisdom when we begin to modify our behaviors. Since change is inevitable, well-managed individuals understand that continual modification is essential to a life well-lived. Modification of any kind leads us to the next frontier of our internal landscape. Just as the agitation of an oyster creates a pearl, these transitions usher us through continual refinement. It is in the process of tumbling and stumbling through upheaval that we discover aspects of Self that ultimately lead to our own liberation. One must only stay open to accepting feedback. That simple orientation, though not easy to do, leads to natural change. It brings about a clarity that can only be experienced when we see the world for what it is instead of what we desire it to be.

Implementation is the act of accountability. Once we consciously commit to managing ourselves, that intention becomes part of our daily lives. Accountability reinforces our understanding of the interdependent nature of our existence. Implementing change in the form of behavior modification is like touching a spider's web: it is impossible to touch one part without affecting the rest. We can think of our internal landscape as the fabric of the time-space continuum. Different thoughts, beliefs, and actions hold different weight and therefore determine the gravitational pull of your life. Once again, education is the awareness that you should make a change. Modification is the preparatory work to make it possible. And implementation is the act of making it manifest.

Every decision we make impacts our internal landscape, as well as the internal landscapes of others. The *educate, modify, implement* feedback loop is a cyclical process of self-refinement similar to the relationship gardeners have with their crops. They understand that sowing seeds in the spring does not automatically lead to a bountiful harvest in the fall. They are eager to enter a relationship with the land—to study nature's patterns, tend to the needs of each plant, and contribute to a larger system. We must approach our lives and landscapes in the same way, to honor the processes of life the same way a gardener stewards the land, with nurturing intent. When we do this, the garden of life supports our every endeavor.

SELF-DISCIPLINE

We find ourselves in the midst of climate change, rampant social injustice, and the sixth mass extinction on planet Earth, because we have lost the ability to govern ourselves through discipline. "Discipline" derives from the Latin verb "to teach" or "to be taught the way to be." Therefore, self-discipline is a creative act of learning and becoming, rather than the constriction many of us associate it with today. Assuming this is a logical response as long as we are conditioned to believe that freedom and discipline reside on opposite ends of the spectrum. It is easy to think that self-discipline will keep us from the carefree life our egos desire or restrict us to the point of rigidity. As with everything, however, life exists on a continuum. Optimal health and wellbeing may shift from one end to the other, but balance is always the ultimate goal.

True discipline arises from our responsibility to develop ourselves and answer a greater calling—to turn inward, dig deep, and design a life that is regenerative in nature. This is our responsibility, our choice, and our destiny. It is our right to create a future designed for the common good. The odds of becoming a human are roughly four hundred trillion to one. Let us remember that we are worthy of that future, not because we have earned it, but simply because we exist.

Discipline does not necessitate drudgery. Nor does it require us to say "no" to everything. Instead, discipline provides the opportunity to say "yes" to what matters most. And early in our journey, discipline is a tool that helps us uncover what matters most.

By now, you may sense that accountability is an area of life that could stand some further development. To awaken our life's core purpose, we must possess the ability to regulate ourselves. Without this, we drift aimlessly and pursue what is most immediately appealing instead of what matters most. It is like looking for the biggest fish in the ocean but only searching the top ten feet of water. We lose depth and mistakenly feel as though mere breadth will replace the profound sacredness we have stripped from life itself.

Waiting for governing bodies and institutions to hold us accountable means losing the opportunity to discover what can only be understood through lived experience. Many of us have lost touch with the self-discipline that enables us to live in harmony with nature. Hubris attempts to excuse us from understanding ourselves as part of a whole, but neither leadership nor unity can be realized without self-discipline. Discipline is the act of synthesizing awareness and reflection as we pursue the proper *way to be*. When we do this, we become firmly rooted on the path toward awakening our life's core purpose.

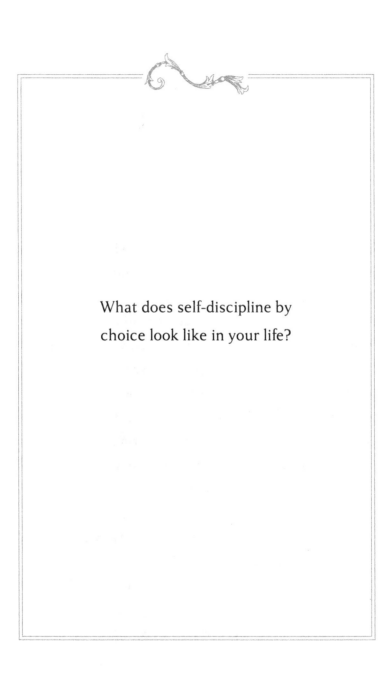

What does self-discipline by
choice look like in your life?

SINGLE-POINTEDNESS

If we are to restore nature, we must reclaim ourselves and hear the calling of the Earth. Howard Thurman once wrote, "Don't ask what the world needs. Ask what makes you come alive and go do it. Because what the world needs is people who have come alive." Similarly, Joseph Campbell said, "I don't think people are looking for the meaning of life so much as they are looking for the experience of being alive." Our greatest opportunity in any lifetime is that of recognizing our core purpose. Each of us has the opportunity to live a life of single-pointedness. This does not mean that life becomes dull, mundane, or limited. Rather, to discover our core purpose is to breathe the breath of the divine and awaken our true nature. It begets simplicity, clarity, and focus as we commune with the deeper meaning of life.

Single-pointedness acts as a magnetic North Pole that draws us inward and simultaneously upward. We are drawn to a space of discernment when we recognize the inherent value of our existence. We act with lovingkindness when we are secure in our base of awareness. We spread joy as others bear witness to our life's core purpose. Single-pointedness allows us to move through life the same way the bow of a ship carves through water. In our wake we leave behind waves of inspiration that ripple outward, impacting everything and everyone around us.

Living our spiritual purpose is the essence of our spiritual lives. Single-pointedness does not mean the highs and lows of life disappear; rather, it raises our supportive floor and promotes stability. It brings joy and equanimity. The concepts of time and linear progress become irrelevant as we recognize that engaging the deep work of self-actualization is ongoing. It has happened for many lifetimes before and will happen for many lifetimes after. We feel secure enough with our internal landscape that we take our eyes off our feet and keep them focused on the path ahead. We gain access to an assuredness that guides our steps and engages us in the surrounding scenery. We bring forth a life rich with meaning and deep in purpose. We come alive.

DISTRACTIONS

Governing oneself is not always easy work, but it can be simple. Eliminating distractions helps us simplify the process of awakening our life's core purpose. However, to do this we must let go of our attachments to those distractions. This can be a challenging task, especially if we are unaware of the attachments in our lives.

As the human race entered the age of information, the age of distraction was not far behind. Distractions can come in an infinite number of forms, but for our purposes, we can think of them as one of two types: internal or external. External distractions are often more self-evident. They may come in the form of a cell phone, a person, or a set of life circumstances. Internal distractions are often more subtle and nuanced in nature. They may come in the form of excuses, a lack of accountability, or coping mechanisms that have become an unconscious crutch. Sometimes, a distraction is as simple as a daydream or the decision to check out. Ultimately, they take our eyes off our compass and lead us astray.

It is not that we must walk the straight and narrow to answer our greater calling. A winding path connects us to insights that are essential for our awakening. However, there is often a fine line between conscious awareness and distractions. The difference between the two is rooted in perception. *The distraction is not the stimuli itself, but rather our attachment to it.* When we divide our attention, we slowly drift from our center. This simple act of shifting away from our center is the distraction itself. By staying centered, we transform distractions into insights that promote spiritual development. Learning to perceive the difference between awareness and distraction brings clarity to our path as we travel toward our true north.

When our attachments result in distraction, they ultimately lead to suffering. Desiring life to be a certain way moves us further from a center that accepts life as it is. When we remain balanced and centered, we can hold distractions in one hand and see the lessons we are meant to learn in the other. We understand they are not mutually exclusive but, instead, intricately connected.

A seedling intuitively senses the importance of remaining rooted as it sprouts from the soil. It must grow leaves and reach tall to access sunlight, but does not abandon its roots along the way. It stays centered. Early in life, the tiny seedling is susceptible to the impact of outside forces. An undisciplined mind is the same, overly susceptible to distractions and fragile in nature. However, the mind that has been cultivated with awareness grows into the mature oak tree. The wind may sway its canopy back and forth, but it remains rooted, centered through its core.

LEARN
YOUR NATURE

The work you have done to learn your true nature takes courage, curiosity, and authenticity. And so, go forth. Be bold. Dive into the waters of wonder and dig into the soil of Self. Know that connecting to your internal landscape is the single most influential thing you can do to promote well-being on this planet. Your conviction to shine light on your path acts as a beacon for others. It is your greatest legacy. The time you spend cultivating awareness and unearthing self-limiting beliefs will generate an undercurrent so strong that a corresponding tsunami of consciousness will envelop your entire being. Allowing those beneficial waves to crash into the shores of others is evolution in action.

Mother Earth generates abundance and resilience, and she encourages connectivity. The same is true for your internal landscape. Openness and adaptability are part of the root system that anchors your soul to satisfaction.

Study yourself and let the awareness you gain dissolve the notion that you are a singular entity existing in a vacuum. It is our own beliefs that isolate us and limit the evolution of our consciousness. Deconstruct the walls you have erected—in the name of self-preservation—that are condemning you to a life of limitations. To be limitless, we must know through experience that the expanse of our internal landscape is infinite. This is the true nature of our existence. Even free will itself becomes irrelevant in the face of our highest purpose and greater calling. We can cultivate any existence we choose, *so let it be an existence of righteousness and virtue.*

SOCIAL LANDSCAPE

DEFINING THE
SOCIAL LANDSCAPE

Our public surroundings and interactions with others comprise the social landscape. While a cultivated mind recognizes the interconnected nature of existence, most of us still perceive the world as divided between inner and outer realms. The opportunity to transcend this belief exists in every interaction. Those on the path of awakening their life's core purpose use awareness to navigate the social landscape effectively.

A cultivated individual understands that challenges in this landscape are merely masked opportunities. Since no two interactions are alike, we may struggle to find a single formula for all our social interactions. Lovingkindness is the single answer we seek. To embody this, awareness guides us toward an inner knowing and helps maintain our identity and integrity in community.

YIN & YANG

The concept of yin and yang is borrowed from Taoism. Again, an in-depth exploration of this philosophy is encouraged but outside the scope of this book. Taosim teaches us that yin and yang are in everything. Yin, a soft and subtle energy, balances yang, a more direct and active energy. Though these energies may be contrary to one another, they are also complementary. One cannot exist without the other. It is the *relationship between* yin and yang that teaches us relativity.

Reviving Indigenous wisdom en masse is the most effective way to reclaim our connection to the natural world. Infusing that wisdom with current technology is the most direct path to planetary health and human wellbeing. Without a contextual understanding of the whole, it is difficult to understand our place inside it. We have mechanized our food system, and simultaneously diminished the diversity our planet needs to thrive. We have generated profound platforms of free speech, and simultaneously created algorithmically constructed echo chambers. We have prioritized intellectual development, and simultaneously eroded the ability to treat one another with compassion. Any amount of give requires take. Any amount of push requires pull. Any amount of growth requires decay. This is simply the way of the world. Mother Earth does not prefer one ecosystem over another; she simply finds the best fit.

Similarly, balance is not always found when we live life in a linear fashion. Staying centered and walking your line does not always mean walking the straight and narrow. Balance is found in the cyclical processes that govern life. Perception defines one's perspective and, ultimately, reality. To the fish underwater, the undercurrent is more impactful than the wave above. To a surfer, the wave itself is all that matters. To the perceptive onlooker, the undercurrent below creates the wave above.

An understanding of yin and yang is essential to the health of our social landscape. It allows us to understand our positionality, or the place we occupy within the greater whole. Ultimately, an informed understanding generates a deeper awareness that guides our interactions in the social landscape. Recognizing the effect the social landscape has on us internally helps us maintain balance when the waters of life get choppy. Instead of trying to decipher between good and bad, we recognize that the distinction itself is an illusion. Yin and yang are relevant to one another only because they make up a singular whole. Similarly, the Earth is a singular whole and we must understand our positioning within her natural law that governs all life.

MARRIAGE OF
EAST & WEST

To sustain the human population on a global scale we must marry the philosophies of East and West. Each has been essential to the evolution of humanity. The innovation of Western culture has connected us in ways that were unthinkable just decades ago. Conversely, the intuitive wisdom of the East and Indigenous communities around the world connect us to ourselves and the Earth in ways Western society struggles to comprehend. Together, they make up the yin and yang of society. A truly aware person honors both.

Western science often promotes the study of the world in its smallest parts. When possible, a detailed understanding of each component creates a detailed understanding of the whole. This is wonderful when it works and useful for categorizing the world around us. Yet it can be easy to lose sight of how an individual component impacts a broader system. One area where this becomes clear is the focus on symptom reduction in Western medicine. This can be helpful if you want to get rid of an earache, but inadequate if you want to learn why they recur and what to do about it. A balanced perspective might ask: what is the heart without blood, lungs without air, or taste buds without food?

On the other hand, Eastern philosophy often places emphasis on the whole, honoring the interdependent nature of life as the foundation of understanding. This awareness of broader systems allows holistic solutions to surface. For example, Eastern medicine often promotes full spectrum wellbeing to avoid the onset of ill health. This approach may seem overly simplistic and not based in facts, but it is undoubtedly rooted in truth: the "outer" world informs our "inner" world and vice versa. The edge zone where Eastern and Western philosophies meet is abundantly fertile.

Socially, it is imperative that we marry Eastern and Indigenous wisdom with Western innovation. We must embrace an intelligence that cannot be quantified and allow the wisdom of intuition to take root in the landscape of Self. As consciousness grows, our ability to receive signals from the environment supports our eye for the minutiae.

By integrating these philosophies, we can create a balanced social landscape, one where our differences manifest as opportunities to strengthen the collective.

IDENTITY & INTEGRITY
IN COMMUNITY

Ultimately, our identities are the root cause of our suffering. If we believe we are separate from the rest of the world, we erect boundaries in the name of self-preservation. This psychological distancing perpetuates fear and anxiety, and, in an attempt to protect ourselves from those emotions, we often retreat further into isolation. The cycle becomes a sort of self-fulfilling prophecy. This is why so many of us feel isolated and disconnected even though there are nearly eight billion people on planet Earth. Certainly, the irony is not lost on you. We perceive separateness, yet we are always and forever bound by connectedness. The nature of yin and yang is always present; we simply fail to align with that truth.

As we wrestle with separation, we must practice self-love and compassion. We must maintain our integrity and allow our identity to remain malleable. It is this receptive disposition that allows us to navigate the back-and-forth nature of the social landscape. If we do not know who we are, how can we find our place within this infinitely diverse space? At the same time, overidentification creates rigidity and weakens the social fabric. It is from this overidentification that extreme phenomena such as cancel culture emerge. We must recognize that authentic identity arises from self-awareness and nonattachment. Integrity is a result of *nonidentity*. "Nonidentity" means that we are open and receptive to life as it is, because we understand that change is the only constant. We know through experience, or awareness, that attaching to a fixed identity ultimately causes pain and suffering.

A fixed mindset manifests in a number of ways societally. We form different sects or social strata in order to make sense of the world. This leads to dehumanization and results in the suffering that so often accompanies isolation. Isolation creates internal wounds; classism creates social wounds; racism creates karmic wounds. *Interconnectedness shows us that inflicting pain on others means inflicting pain on ourselves.*

Therefore, to heal ourselves and one another, we must see ourselves as inextricably linked. Though we have never met, my wellbeing while penning these words is directly connected to your wellbeing while reading them. The dance of duality orchestrates the interdependent nature of life. For that dance to go smoothly, both partners must be in sync. Diversity creates resilience in the natural world, and it also stitches the fabric of the social landscape, allowing us to reach across the aisle and dance with a stranger. Interdependence means we must embrace our differences and dissolve our identities to embody true integrity.

We need not become a uniform society, but rather embrace the fact that we are a homogeneous species. Humans must learn to coexist the same way that predator and prey coexist. The eagle and the fish do not interact continuously to hash out their differences and become one. Instead, they allow one another to coexist. Should the eagle decide to hunt fish to the brink of extinction, it would soon realize its interdependence on the fish for its own survival. You may ask yourself, "What does the fish get out of all of this?" Once caught, as it soars with the eagle above the water and sees the landscape below, it gains a new perspective as it transitions to a new life. Indeed, the fish may receive the greatest gift of all: embracing a life after death that is not bound by the limitations of the lake and not determined by the physical nature of its existence. The fish receives an opportunity to fully transcend this plane, and its final offering is an act of service. Yin after yang, life after death. What more could any of us ask for?

SEPARATE THE WHEAT
FROM THE CHAFF

Awareness reveals one of the greatest opportunities: living a life of service. Here, the cyclical nature of life is revealed again. To be of service to another is also to be in service of Self, and to be of service to Self extends our capacity to serve others. Each part of a plant is essential for its survival. Society is the same. Whether we understand or recognize this is irrelevant—natural order remains. It is the plant's ability to work in unison with itself that produces fruit at season's end. The roots need not manage the stem and the leaves; they must only trust them to do their part. We must trust one another and demonstrate an ability to live in such a way that allows everyone to pursue their life's core purpose.

Each of us must determine what is most essential for our growth and development. As we apply the awareness gained from self-study, we learn how to manage ourselves within the larger context of the social landscape. We begin to see our role in serving the greater whole. Perhaps we are soil, rich with minerals providing nutrients for others. Perhaps we are water, taking the path of least resistance and nourishing the landscape. Perhaps we are air, silent and unseen, but offering the molecules that make life possible. Perhaps we are the warmth of the sun, the shade of a tree, or a songbird's melody. This understanding shows us that we are all essential. Our only responsibility is to do our part to the best of our abilities.

Separating the wheat from the chaff is an opportunity to streamline our purpose and trim away the excess in search of our true essence. But the chaff is not useless once the wheat is harvested. It is added to the compost and made into fertilizer for next year's crop. *Mutuality and respect bind us to the greater whole.* A wise person senses that what seems irrelevant today may become relevant tomorrow; a virtuous person knows that all is relevant all the time. This holistic awareness leads us to reverence for all beings and service to the social landscape.

BOUNDARIES & KEEPING
WITH GOOD ENERGY

Self-awareness and boundaries work together like a plant's roots exchanging carbon for nutrients in the soil. Boundaries act as mycorrhizae, the gatekeepers that enable us to communicate our needs, choose what we let in, and decide what to keep out. Boundaries can be applied to anything in our physical, social, mental, emotional, or spiritual proximity. They are an opportunity to design our relationships as catalysts for positive change. It does not mean that we separate ourselves from the rest of the world. Rather, we transform our relationships through conscious intent. *This process often requires a great deal of emotional vulnerability.*

Our energy is the most precious resource we have, and cultivating it is essential. The social landscape impacts us emotionally, socially, and somatically. Once we commit consciously to awakening our life's core purpose, the need to set boundaries becomes self-evident. We know when a boundary is healthy, because it resonates at our core and provides energy to pursue our true north. Keeping with good energy transforms our social landscape and creates space in our lives to resonate at a higher frequency. When this happens, we become a lighthouse for others who are lost in the dark.

When a sculptor makes marks in the clay, he can sense when it is becoming too dry and rigid or too soft and supple. He understands the boundaries of the clay and learns to work with them. If we have a vision, in the form of our true north, we can live our life in an intentional direction. If not, we can allow the form to be revealed in a simple and accepting manner. Neither method is better or worse than the other. It is the creative process that matters most. The sculptor teaches us that navigating the social landscape requires us to be neither too loose nor too rigid in our boundaries.

A healthy social landscape raises the collective consciousness the same way a lock-and-dam system raises water levels. Just as water in the dam will seek its own level, so will the energy of society. Once something or someone has entered our awareness, it becomes our responsibility to understand how it impacts our energy. Like an owl surveying the land from its perch in the trees, our awareness feels for the subtle differences in our energy that show us healthy boundaries. Setting those boundaries is like putting up the guard rails on our spiritual path. Keeping with good energy allows us to increase our wellbeing while we elevate the social landscape around us.

FAMILY
SELECTION

It is often said that we do not choose our family. This could not be further from the truth. The soul is sentient and understands what it needs to continue its evolution. It then chooses those circumstances with great purpose. If we acknowledge that consciousness begins before birth, we can see the painter as she prepares the canvas, not just the finished product. We can hear the orchestra within the mind of the conductor as he selects sheet music, not just the final performance. Keeping with good energy is a matter of choice. This includes selecting a family that supports the evolution of our soul and the pursuit of a greater calling.

Our biological family in this lifetime is not our only family. Indeed, some of us never know our blood relations. Therefore, we can design our family the same way we design our internal landscape. This process gives us more influence over the structure of our family than most people take credit for. Family is not fixed; it evolves just like anything else. As the vining plant climbs, does it know its precise destination or is it simply seeking sunlight? We must grow in the same fashion, setting our intention toward the sun and embracing the journey along the way.

Yet we must also honor our roots, or the family circumstances our soul chose at birth. The conditions we grew up with provide insight into the aspects of ourselves that need healing. For example, the stability of your childhood might now encourage you to take risks. Or your journey through foster care inspires you to cultivate a loving home within yourself. Maybe losing a parental figure early in life now motivates you to fully individuate. Or perhaps the abuse you experienced as a child leads to the healing your soul yearns for. These early experiences and our responses to them are the soul seeking justice through healing. The same way the vine trusts the process of ascension, we trust the intelligence of a Higher Self.

Remember, there is reason in everything that happens. However, those reasons may not be revealed without a bit of soul searching. When we say this flippantly without examination, we miss an opportunity to align ourselves with the justice our soul seeks. Ultimately, this is a disservice to ourselves and others as well.

If we want to be healers in the world, we must be able to heal ourselves. If we want to shine light in the world, we must bear light within us. If we long for connection, we must find ways to connect with ourselves. And if we desire to see unity in the world, then we must reclaim that unity internally.

Reflect on your family experience both
early in life and throughout your life.

- What does that reflection
  process teach you?

- How has it shaped the person
  you have become?

- How does it inform your direction
  in life moving forward?

SIGNIFICANT OTHERS

Intimate relationships are a great mirror for ourselves and the social landscape. Love is always expressed from the inside out. When we experience love from others, it is because they have love within themselves. When we find connection with others, it provides us an opportunity to connect with ourselves. If you long for intimacy but have been unable to find or sustain it, then you must start from where you are. Reflect deeply about your own internal love and connectedness. To find what you are looking for, determine what self-actualization you require. And remember the words of the great poet Rumi, "What you seek is seeking you."

A significant other offers an ever-present opportunity to live from the heart space. This is an essential skill if we desire to awaken purpose and be of service. Body consciousness shows us what it feels like to live from the heart space. It also teaches us about mutuality in relationships. In nature, a rock provides substrate for the moss and lichen that cover it. Such a relationship requires the right environmental conditions as well as a willingness to give and receive. It also requires a delicacy that an untrained mind and undisciplined heart struggle to invoke. Living from the heart is a way of *being* and an evolutionary process. Devotion to that process reveals aspects of our internal landscape that inform our growth and development.

Even in the anaerobic conditions of a wetland, life still finds a way. We must create the conditions that allow us to love. We must oxidize our hearts when they become bogged down with the anaerobic conditions of selfishness and disease. Courageous conversations and vulnerability are cornerstones to a committed relationship. Let your significant other know your true feelings. Know that you will be hurt and remember that it is no reason to stop loving. It is the determination of love itself that allows life to spring forth in the most adverse conditions and unexpected ways. It is often here, in our relationships, that we cross the Rubicon of Self and move from our minds to our hearts. Let love lead the way, and learn to adapt like a vine determining its path toward the sun.

THE GRACE OF
GRIEF & LOSS

The natural world has perfected the art of turning death into new life. When a plant or animal dies, it does not exit the circle of life. Rather, all living things, including ourselves, return to a space of reclamation before reincarnation. Death is the transformational change that allows us to ascend to our purest form. It is the unknown that causes us to fear it. Connecting with a higher perspective will show us the grace of grief and loss, which is essential for cultivating a compassionate social landscape.

Everyone experiences loss. It may be the loss of a family member, significant other, or, more abstractly, the benevolence from our childhood. No matter the circumstance, what is most important is our perspective surrounding it. If we choose to see it as something that brings only pain and suffering, that will assuredly be our reality. However, if we search for both the yin and yang, an alternative perspective is revealed. Instead of suffering, and in addition to the pain, we can embrace all the lessons loss has to teach us.

When we perceive the world from an either-or vantage point, we start to believe that life itself is mutually exclusive. This leads to separation and, ultimately, disease. At the root of this disconnectedness lies the rigidity of human perception. An unexpected loss can completely alter life, and in that moment, we are often devastated. We make matters worse when we expect the world to unfold in a linear fashion. When we experience loss, we must acknowledge our pain and also sense beyond it. What are we meant to learn from the loss? If we remain open, and grounded in awareness, we will see its divine orchestration in time. Ultimately, the art of letting go is an essential lesson to learn and a crucial tool in our tool belt.

When we see ourselves as separate from the rest of the world, we take things personally and make losses about *our* experience as opposed to *the* experience. This brings discomfort and disillusionment. However, when we let go of our attachments, we are like the experienced meditator watching their thoughts come and go. We understand that grief and loss are simply fellow travelers on the journey of life. They come and go just like life itself. Therefore, we do not need to form attachments or wrap ourselves up in the pain and suffering that so often accompany loss. And though we hold space for our emotions, we learn that letting go allows us to overcome.

Take time to reflect on your experiences of grief and loss. Search for grace. Believe there is wisdom in seeing through the rustling leaves that keep you from looking directly at your pain. Your experience flows just like a river. The loss you are holding on to will float downstream if you are willing to let go. The same can be said for your perceptions and beliefs. You may be holding on to relics of the past that stunt your growth and development. Hold space for the emotions that accompany your loss and move forward as you are able. Letting go does not mean losing out; every experience from our past shapes our journey ahead. Give yourself permission to let go and allow the cosmos to fill that newfound space in life.

SELF-AWARENESS
BEGETS SIMPLICITY

Simplicity emerges on our quest to awaken our life's core purpose. As we begin to see the nuances of the social landscape, we also see how they relate to our internal landscape. This awareness develops within you, and the world begins to simplify. Simplicity is not a destination we navigate toward, but rather a state of existence we operate from. Like us, nature is a complex system, and also like us, a simple purpose perpetuates its self-awareness: the drive for life.

The more we practice self-awareness, the easier it is to simplify our experience of the world around us. We see snags in our internal landscape but avoid getting tripped up by them. We see snares in the social landscape but elude them. We release our attachments and hold healthy boundaries to keep with good energy. Though it may feel like we are distancing ourselves from the world, the subtle truth is that we are coming to know the world more intimately. We can observe the landscape centered on our sitting post just as well as exploring it by foot.

If we allow it to be, life is simple. When we take the time to cultivate ourselves, we begin to understand that it does not take much to satisfy the soul. We see the role we are meant to play in the social landscape, the same way a carpenter ant understands its place in the colony. We need not question it. Holding our mind in a certain kind of way simplifies life and keeps our awareness fixed on our higher purpose. However, when we succumb to base instincts, our attention focuses right in front of our feet, and shortsightedness ensues. It is more enjoyable to allow the feet to navigate the path under-foot and keep our eyes on the horizon. Watching with the eyes yet following something else with the mind trains our awareness to see the bigger picture. The more we maintain this equilibrium, the simpler the human realm becomes.

Our centeredness provides a holistic view of reality that elevates our awareness beyond what is right in front of our feet. We see and sense distractions for what they are and respond accordingly. We recognize human nature for what it is and understand what it has to offer. *In many ways, self-awareness is the soil of spirituality.* When we know our soil, our spiritual life simplifies, and in turn the social landscape will benefit.

CENTER
& RESET

Inevitably, we will sway from our center and fall from our sitting post. When this happens, our task at hand is to regain that centeredness. The natural law of balance calls us back to center. This reorientation allows us to travel what the Buddhist tradition calls the Middle Way, or a life that avoids extremes, and this path leads us to our life's core purpose. To continuously center and reset liberates us from our base instincts and keeps us connected to our greater calling. Our expectations become openness as we travel the path toward our true north.

Awareness, body consciousness, and conscious commitment allow us to center and reset. When the social landscape distracts us, we stop, breathe, and regain our composure. This is a skill we must rehearse time and again, but eventually it becomes second nature. At first, it requires all our effort and intention. We have become so conditioned to fill every void, heal every wound, and satiate every desire that life has become an endless cycle of seeking instead of a consistent practice of being. We have entered an endless dance, chasing our own tail. To exit this dance, we must center and reset.

When the zebra outpaces the cheetah, it does not run to tell all its friends, nor does it perseverate on its fear. Rather, when the cheetah is a safe distance away, the zebra shakes and shudders its body. When the chase is done, the chase is done. The zebra does not carry its fear into the future. Instead, it trusts its instincts to recognize danger when it is present, and spends the rest of its time grazing the plains, grounded in the present moment. The zebra literally centers and resets its nervous system. So many humans have forgotten the practice, or have never been taught. To reclaim this ability at scale, we must first practice it as individuals until it becomes as natural for us as it is for the zebra.

To center and reset, we do not need to shake compulsively; we only need to connect with the breath consciously. This consciousness allows us to recognize our higher calling as a species. When we escape the clutches of desire, we are able to commune with our true nature. A thorough exploration of our inner landscape reveals our center. From there, it is our responsibility to stay tethered to it as we navigate the social landscape. There are many distractions that can knock us off-center. In the end, we should thank them, as they give us the opportunity to center and reset.

RESILIENCE

We often interpret resilience as the ability to endure—a conviction so unwavering that nothing can knock it off-center—but this is an incomplete understanding. Sometimes resilience does require persistence and perseverance. More importantly, however, resilience demands flexibility and adaptation. *Resilience is the ability to navigate life's circumstances with agility and to recover with ease.* A tree will eventually snap if a strong enough force pushes against it, whereas seaweed flows and flexes even as the water rages all around. Their true strength comes from yielding. The tree sways back and forth in the wind, and the seaweed sways back and forth in the water.

Awakening our life's core purpose requires resilience. However, we do not need to feel like a salmon swimming upstream; resilience may also look like an otter floating on its back. The difference between firmness and agility is largely a difference in energy. We attract experiences that are meant to teach us what we need to learn most. If we define strength as an unyielding force, life will present events that test our resolve. Ultimately, we must learn to adapt and flow with the energy of the cosmos.

Awareness and responsiveness are the backbone of resilience. The grazers of the Great Plains do not stand stubbornly when there is no food underfoot; they move to greener pastures. The black bear does not stay awake for winter; it welcomes hibernation. The school of sardines does not swim in rank formation; they expand and contract as a single cloud-like organism. It is our task to become vast and diverse, yet agile and adaptive. We should flow, rather than resist; accept, rather than challenge; center and reset, rather than persevere. The way to a cohesive society is through each individual functioning as an integral part of the whole.

SOCIAL JUSTICE

We cannot discuss the social landscape without mentioning social justice and cultural competency. Social and environmental justice are two wings of the same bird. It is not coincidental that the largest social justice movement since the 1960s—Black Lives Matter—coincided with a greater awakening to climate collapse. The separation and disconnect that we experience internally manifests in the social and external landscapes. *The disease of separateness drives a wedge between ourselves and others, the Earth, and the divine; it is the taproot of humanity's plight.*

Social justice is often portrayed as a movement forward. Yet, it is this push forward that has stripped the soil from humanity's spirit. The West marks the beginning of the modern era with the invention of the plow. This revolutionary tool marked a turning point in our relationship to the land. Natural coexistence turned into domination as Westerners began to manipulate natural law. In the process, the notion arose that we could control the environment. In the quest to take control of the ecological systems that govern biological life, the equally oppressive belief that it was necessary to govern one another persisted in the minds of some.

We quite literally plowed under the fabric of society that allowed the human species to coexist naturally for thousands of years, replacing it with an intellectual pursuit deemed superior to antiquated paradigms. Bear in mind that a natural coexistence does not mean a peaceful coexistence. Human conflict did not originate after the plow. However, the drive to dominate the Earth perpetuated a collective control paradigm. In spite of this, yin and yang continue to create balance in all things, and this reveals a fundamental truth about our relationship to the land, one that has been well understood by Indigenous cultures for millennia: *we can influence but we cannot control.*

Of course, we must not permit inequality, exploitation, and systemic oppression of people and the Earth. Indeed, we must accept that these challenges exist and recognize our collective responsibility to do something constructive about them. There has always been competition, which is healthy so far as it spurs growth and creativity. But it has its place, just like everything else. Competition without compassion can quickly turn insidious. It can only be healthy if it remains within the domain of natural law. When we move forward with haste, we miss the wisdom that only patience reveals. Nature does not push forward; rather, it is pulled by the methodical wheel of evolution. Though society must be radically transformed, a collective awareness must also guide the process of change ahead.

What does this have to do with social justice? Western paradigms reason that competition is required to distribute the "natural resources" Mother Earth offers. But how is that process of distribution working? With the technological advancements and economic resources available to us, well over half the planet still lives in abject poverty. We might then seek to understand the causes of poverty, but the solution to this crisis is rooted within the problem. An infinite growth paradigm that exists outside the bounds of natural law, on a planet with finite "resources," results in a mad scramble for power in the name of survival. That mad scramble distributes power unequally, and capital of all kinds is then concentrated in the hands of a select few.

It should be clarified that those "resources" are only made finite because of our orientation to them. If we insist on mining, fracking, and drilling for the sake of extraction, then those resources are indeed finite. If we remain dependent upon the companies who control those "resources," then we indeed perpetuate the problem. *However, if we reorient our relationship to consumption and explore the many ways to coexist with the natural world, we quickly discover that the Earth's willingness to provide is infinite.*

Perhaps we have neglected to apply human ingenuity at scale to develop a sustainable society. Many believe the world is overpopulated, and this is true if we remain committed to the current models of industrial agricultural and energy production. Indeed, there are not enough wild places if we insist on deforestation in the name of "cultivation." Yet, with all these myopic mistakes, why does the Earth continue to provide and be so forgiving? We need not condemn those who have perpetuated these systems that devastate Mother Earth. We must only commit ourselves to an alternative path, one that embraces a willingness to live with what we *truly* need and to share our bounty with anyone who knocks at our door.

The great irony is that to go forward, we must return to our roots. We must restore the external landscape and restitch the fabric of society. We must recognize our responsibility to save ourselves and allow ourselves to be saved. We must create the conditions that allow an alternative paradigm to emerge that fosters compassion and encourages co-creation. This is not to deny the violent history of humanity that existed long before the plow. Rather, it is to suggest that our push forward encourages the Earth to push back.

The desire for control has deconstructed the fabric of society by disenfranchising billions. Western mechanisms used for cultivation were developed alongside the same technologies used to enslave Black people and commit the genocide of Indigenous peoples worldwide. Now, a modern-day movement to control the Earth threatens life for countless species. The movements of social and ecological justice are challenging the same machine of oppression that emerged from Western colonialism. While this is not an argument that we need new initiatives, it *is* a call to uproot the segregation and dissociation so deeply ingrained within so many of us.

There is wisdom in the voice of the Earth. The communities fluent in the language of her tongue possess the knowledge to architect a path forward. The Ghanaian term "Sankofa" conveys the importance of reaching back for past knowledge to create progress in the present. This wisdom reveals that all we need exists within us. These solutions have been buried deep within our psyche. Bringing them forth will require collective effort. *The simplest answer for ecological restoration is to let the Earth rest.* However, to restore the social landscape, we cannot remain passive! Retribution, restitution, and reparations will all be required before reconciliation is possible. Instead of searching for the land of moral superiority, we might instead look inward and own our dissonance. We must find our path among men, among the angels, among the stars, and follow in the footsteps of the light. By reviving ourselves, we can live in unity with the Earth once again.

LEARN
FROM NATURE

As Western society separated itself from the Earth conceptually, it also separated itself from the wisdom of nature. This is not a novel concept; Indigenous cultures around the world have long spoken this truth as part of their spiritual identities. Therefore, many of us must accept that we bought into a cultural paradigm that is fundamentally flawed. Moreover, we must embrace native ways of knowing. It may feel as though we are trapped once again within the confines of natural law. But the question must be asked: did we ever escape it to begin with? *Not only does nature hold the answer; nature is the answer.*

The cosmos has an inherent drive to expand, and part of that expansion involves a mysticism that cannot be defined. But this drive is present within the social landscape. The solutions are already in front of us should we choose to drink from the stream of the Great Mystery. We must design social systems that mimic the patterns of nature. We must succumb to the wisdom of the unseen and the unspoken. We must allow the omnipotence of the feminine archetype to be revealed in all that we do. It is the mother who gives birth to the child. It is Mother Earth who gives birth to life itself. We must draw upon lessons from the Earth to guide our path toward an inclusive social landscape for all.

We are simply an extension of evolution, a limb on the great Tree of Life, a finger of God with the responsibility to embody the divine nature of existence. Our lust for comprehension must evolve into a craving for compassion and curiosity. Only then will we be able to transform the culture of civilization. Instead of seeking to understand, we can simply surrender. Instead of furrowing the brow, we can simply smile. Instead of distancing ourselves, we can simply unite. Indeed, this is a tall task. Yet Earth does not require nearly eight billion people to realize this all at once. *We need not awaken the masses; we must only awaken ourselves.*

Each of us has the opportunity to help bring the human race to critical mass, to move our existence beyond sustainability. It will require realignment, but the reconstruction has already begun. All that is asked of us is to find our place in that evolutionary process and take a single step. As the ancient Chinese proverb states, "The journey of a thousand miles begins with a single step." Find your rhythm and walk in sync with your life's core purpose. Recognize that you are exactly where you are meant to be. When the statistical probability of our existence is so small, how can we not embrace a mysticism that is so vast? Seek truth in nature. Place your roots deep and strong. Trust that you are wholly without sin and draw upon the Earth to expand your truth.

SECTION THREE

EXTERNAL LANDSCAPE

DEFINING THE
EXTERNAL LANDSCAPE

The external landscape, or natural world, makes all life on Earth possible. It also teaches us a great deal about our internal landscapes, which vibrate in harmony with nature. In our minds and hearts we must recognize the external landscape as the backdrop of our existence and the foreground of our growth. This is essential in our journey from soil to spirit if we desire to remain a spoke in the grand wheel of evolution.

Much has been said regarding the external landscape already. However, specific attention must be paid to the natural world to anchor our understanding. Much like our spiritual center within, the Earth stores solutions to any challenge we face. From the smell of a cedar tree to the mineral composition of quartz, from the call of a songbird to the tonal frequency of a whale, the opportunity to experience Earth's grace is truly boundless. Liberating our internal landscape will allow us to heal society and coexist peacefully in the natural world. The harmony created from those processes, like ripples in a pond, extends outward and impacts the spiritual landscape.

LEARN
FROM HISTORY

Paradoxically, by looking backward, we can see a path forward. History provides insight to guide the evolution of Homo sapiens. To study the rise and fall of civilizations is to reveal our own threats in the present day. Whether war, famine, economics, or natural disasters, the reasons for societal collapse are numerous. Yet, many are caused by the human hand, a perceived lack of resources for survival, and the deconstruction of the social fabric.

When there is an overabundance of resources, there is a natural pull to create more life to restore balance. When there is a restriction of resources, there is a restriction of life itself. This points us to a solution that exists between the ink and the paper, between the voice and the ear, between the roots and the soil. Our task is not to seek methods of production that outpace our consumption. *Rather, our responsibility is to design a way of life that keeps us suspended in equilibrium with the natural rhythms of the Earth.* We must design internal, external, and social landscapes that provide for all life, coexisting with the natural world and learning from her wisdom, guided by the unseen and unspoken. We must live in such a way that the collective footprint of the human species is generative, not extractive.

Extractive systems self-impose their own demise. In the natural world, it is impossible to sustain a system that is not conducive to life itself. Therefore, as the leaders of society propose solutions to the challenges we face, it is our responsibility to evaluate those solutions within the context of what is best for all. If we leave the choice in the hands of the powerful, we are destined to receive solutions that favor the few and ostracize many. Such a path forward will lead to greater social discord, creating even greater challenges for future generations.

TURN TO NATURE

The Earth distributes resources with an awareness of what is mutually beneficial for all beings on Earth. The microbes and bacteria bring the soil to life, the soil anchors the plant kingdom, plants provide nourishment for animals, death feeds the microbes in the soil, and the cycle continues. Every aspect of nature holds its place in the external landscape. Similarly, every individual holds their place in society, and every soul holds its place in the individual. As Lao Tzu once wrote, "Nature does not rush, yet everything is accomplished." The Earth trusts in her process of evolution, and we too must trust that our capabilities will lead us to great destinations in this world and beyond. We must remain responsible in this stage of exploration and know that everything will be accomplished in time.

Our responsibility in this cycle is only to govern ourselves. The squirrel does not tell the oak tree when to drop its acorns; he simply enjoys the fruits of the tree's labor. The worm does not tell the plant when to die; it simply creates organic matter for others to thrive. The baby does not tell her mother how to care for her; she simply receives that care and provides feedback when needed. Embracing this natural ebb and flow brings us into harmony with nature. Internal alignment makes social alignment possible.

As the social landscape aligns, it naturally syncs with cycles governed by the external landscape. However, this is not necessarily a linear process. What's most important is our recognition that the natural world aligns us with a taproot to the divine. From the microbes in soil to solar systems within galaxies, all are governed by natural law.

NATURAL LIVING

The Earth has shown us that if we do not abide by natural law, we will be ostracized from her kingdom. We only come to terms with our insatiability when we understand this truth. It is impossible for us to sustain our own existence as a species without a natural way of life. What's more, this natural way of life is what we desire. Our deepest need as human beings is to belong. Excess production and consumption are distractions that lead us astray and sever our connection to the Earth and the divine.

Is it any wonder that humans suffer from widespread chronic illness at this time? While there are more people on the planet now than ever before, overpopulation does not necessarily mean more disease. As scientists themselves might argue, correlation is not causation. We must look deeper to find the cause. Many of us are as distant from the Earth as we have ever been, and this disconnect leads to a poor foundation for health and skyrocketing rates of chronic illness.

The argument over nature versus nurture has long been settled: it is undoubtedly nature *and* nurture. The time has come for us to nurture our own internal nature, to commune and sit by the fire of the Great Mother Earth. She provides all the warmth and sustenance that we will ever need, and all the mysticism that our souls could ever want. Let us revive our commitment to the commons through curiosity and connection. Let us lean into the benevolent teachers who act as shepherds along the path. Let us stay grounded in awareness as we discover energies that seek to guide our emergence onto the universal field.

PERMACULTURE

Permaculture is a regenerative design philosophy typically associated with the design of agricultural systems that mimic those in nature. It recognizes the Earth as the most intelligent teacher and suggests that biomimicry is our best course of action. It is built on three foundational ethics: care of people, care of Earth, and care of the future (or "fair share"). Accompanying those ethics are twelve design principles that outline a multifaceted approach to restoration and regeneration. Again, it is outside the scope of this book to cover all twelve principles, but additional reading on the subject is encouraged.

Purists in the field believe that permaculture should only be used to create organic, living systems. Though their reasoning is sound, the world needs sustainable solutions across the entire spectrum of human existence—materially, socially, internally, and spiritually. Can the environment truly flourish if we are unable to coexist with one another and the Earth?

Can we design prosperous societies if we are unable to cultivate our own inner landscapes? Furthermore, what will all of this mean if we fall out of touch with the true nature of our existence? Will we be able to maintain a natural equilibrium with ourselves, one another, and planet Earth if we do not see and sense our greater calling?

Without that connection to ourselves and a higher purpose, the answer is assuredly no. The ethics and design principles of permaculture can allow us to shape a future for all. We must embrace our interdependence and stay open to new ways of being. We must notice the subtleties of life and pay attention to the lessons therein. We *inhabit* the world. We are not living *on* this planet; we are living *in* this planet.

The philosophical underpinnings of permaculture acknowledge this truth. The only path toward a truly sustainable future and perma(nent)culture is to live within systems that abide by the natural laws of the Earth. There will be perils and rewards as we journey toward atonement. Our responsibility is to live discerningly, in such a way that we care for people, the planet, and the future.

NATURE-BASED
THERAPEUTICS

Nature-Based Therapeutics, or the study of nature's healing capacities, explores the link between human health and
nature. Though the field is young, the findings are overwhelmingly clear: our relationship to nature is essential to
our wellbeing. Nature has inherent therapeutic qualities that
impact our physiology, psychology, and sociology. We know
that nature restores attention, soothes the sympathetic nervous system, and even promotes prosocial behavior. Entire
volumes have been dedicated to this field of study and do not
need duplication here. Instead, we will explore its relevance
to soil and spirit.

Organisms function through the sum of their parts, and
the Earth is part of our sum total. The physical landscape
is undoubtedly an integral component of our wellbeing as
a species. To take care of ourselves, we must be able to take

care of one another. To take care of one another, we must be able to take care of the Earth. And to take care of the Earth, we must honor our connection to her. Without this awareness, we will miss the mark and travel away from our collective true north.

If we rely on traditional Western science to prove that nature is essential to our wellbeing, we distance ourselves from the intuitive capacities that allow us to discover this truth for ourselves. From the child who explores the sensory experience of soil to the elder who spent their lifetime observing the cycles of the seasons, each senses the wonder and delight provided by the natural world. The need for proof reveals how truly myopic we have become. Climate collapse declares that we do not have time for governing bodies, organizations, and institutions to orchestrate an ecological recovery through policy alone. We are in need of individuals who see the connection and live out their purpose for others to witness. Among other things, the field of Nature-Based Therapeutics offers validity to worldwide conservation efforts. But it does not need to be verified to validate our reverence for the natural world.

There is no need to wait for science to prove what our hearts and heads already know to be true. *Human health is impossible without nature.* Perhaps more importantly, humans are not essential to nature's health. We are simply another species to emerge from Earth's evolutionary process, and without careful consideration, we will be lost to history along with all the other species we have pushed past the brink of extinction. Let us embrace the scientific validity of Nature-Based Therapeutics and integrate the wisdom our souls know to be true. Let us revive eco-reverence worldwide.

NATURE ANALOGIES TO UNDERSTAND THE INNER LANDSCAPE

Since we are natural beings made of the natural world, there are many parallels we can draw between us and Mother Earth. Below is a set of analogies meant to reveal just how closely connected we are. Some are science-based, and others are simply concepts to stir deeper reflection. May they promote a more nuanced understanding of life, love, and nature within you.

LAYERS OF SELF

There are different layers in a forest. Each layer offers different microclimates for plants and animals to inhabit. The Self is similar. We have many layers that we might perceive as depth. To do the deep work of awakening our life's core purpose, it is imperative that we dive to the depths of Self. This is why awakening, or spiritual ascension, can also be viewed as a process of descension. As we navigate our internal land-scape, we must look up, down, and side to side, while examining what lies beneath the surface.

Forest Layers	Correlation to Self
7. Canopy	7. Highest Self: our life's core purpose aligned with the divine
6. Sub-canopy	6. Best Self: self that requires discipline and conscious intent
5. Shrub and Herbaceous	5. Common Self: who we are during our regular day-to-day lives
4. Vertical or Climbing	4. Developing Self: self that we are in the midst of developing
3. Ground Cover	3. Foundational Self: our daily routines, behaviors, interactions, etc.
2. Mycelial and Fungal Layer	2. Communicative Self: our physiological self; body awareness
1. Soil	1. Bedrock Self: our core beliefs and values; our identity and integrity

SOIL & SELF

In nature, soil is largely responsible for the health of an ecosystem, and healthy soil is composed of many elements. Topsoil emerges from the subsoil, which emerges from the bedrock below. Sand, silt, clay, and organic matter represent the foundation of fertility and health. A soil that is barren and dead became that way because of misuse and abuse, but it can be nourished. By adding nutrients and organic matter in the form of diverse experiences, self-care, compassion, and understanding, we add life to our inner soils. The healthier we are below the surface, the healthier we can show up in the world around us.

	Structure of Soil	Structure of Self
Sand	rock and mineral particles (largest size): *porous, does not hold water well*	well drained, porous, and flexible: *aspects of self that are "easy going"*
Silt	granular sediment deposits (medium size): *substantial sediment deposits can cause buildups*	sediment carried by water and deposited elsewhere: *if left unattended too long, will cause unwanted blockages*
Clay	fine-grained materials (smallest size): *rich in nutrients, water-holding capacity*	when waterlogged, nutrients become unavailable: *aspects of self that are "non-negotiable" and inflexible*
Organic Matter	organic carbon-based organisms: *best way to improve soil fertility is to add organic matter*	organic fertilizer, improves vitality and resiliency: *aspects of self that are "life giving" in nature, generative*
Water	Analogous to our attention and intentions; aspects of life that move us in a particular direction	
Loamy Soil	The unique combination of the three elements sand, silt, and clay is referred to as a "loam soil."	
Ratio	Ideal soil structure is 40:40:20 sand, silt, and clay with high organic matter.	

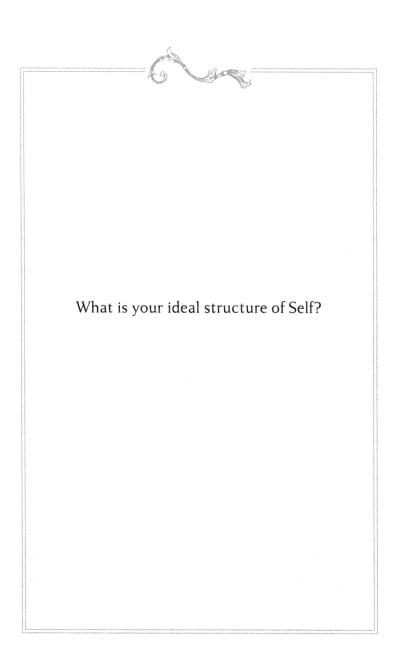

What is your ideal structure of Self?

MICROORGANISMS

Soil is filled with microorganisms, bacteria, viruses, and fungi. The health of the soil heavily impacts the health of the plants, which directly affects the health of our gut microbiome. A healthy community of microorganisms equates to a functional soil biology, resulting in a well-balanced foundation upon which we design our internal landscape. Microorganisms can be viewed as foundational building blocks that make up the whole of life's experiences, both internally, externally, and socially. Every experience we encounter is some form of stimulus that impacts the health of our soil. Often, like microorganisms, these stimuli are imperceptible at the surface. But when we examine them closely, we can see how they impact us at a microscopic level. Well-balanced soil creates resilience and immunity in the process of self-cultivation.

MYCELIUM

Fungi are nature's fiber-optic cables. A mycelial web is a vast underground communication network capable of sending messages across great distances. Internally, we have our own communication networks, as well. In the brain, neurons allow communication across synaptic gaps. In the body, cells communicate with other cells around them. In the stomach, the gut lining delivers molecules into the bloodstream. This communication results in a single, unified, functioning organism. Even at the molecular and cellular levels, we are truly intelligent beings. Communicating internal messages of love, compassion, health, and vitality reinforces signals within our bodies that promote those exact outcomes. Rehearsing negative self-talk, emotional patterns, and judgment reinforces conditions that constrict personal and spiritual growth. What type of internal landscape are you cultivating as you communicate with your surroundings consciously and unconsciously?

MYCORRHIZAE

Plants are opportunistic; they take root in soil that is conducive to their survival. That survival is also dependent upon mycorrhizae. These are fungal structures that colonize plant roots and enable the exchange of nutrients between roots and soil. We possess our own mycorrhizae-like structures within our internal landscape. Envision the body's innate intelligence network that allows different systems, such as the circulatory, respiratory, and digestive systems, to function in concert with one another. Optimal self-management requires this exchange of nutrients and information. The soil we have cultivated internally determines which nutrients we are able to provide for the plants that have taken root in our garden. If we attempt to sow seeds of love and unity but have not diversified our own internal soil biology, these seeds may struggle to take root. Therefore, we must pay attention to the soil of Self if we desire to grow a garden with conscious intent.

ROOTS

Plants have adapted to get their nutrients from the soil, water, air, or even insects. But regardless of how they function, roots typically take up nutrients and anchor the plant to its surroundings. If the root structure of a plant is unhealthy or disturbed, it affects the entire plant—as above, so below. The same is true for the Self. Think of roots as the internal aspects of Self that anchor us. If we allow honesty, integrity, and curiosity to germinate within us, we cultivate a root structure conducive to growth. If we water seeds of doubt, fear, and shame, personal development and spiritual maturation will be hard to come by. Our roots anchor us to our foundation and help shape our integrity.

TAPROOT

Some plants have a taproot. Instead of a root structure resembling the canopy of the plant, they send a single main root down to anchor into the Earth. We have taproots, as well. For example, if you respond with anger when someone cuts you off on the road, you may *fear* what would happen if there were to be an accident. In this scenario, fear is the taproot that feeds the many branches of expression. When we find undesirables in our gardens, such as dandelions or burdock, we must be mindful when removing them, making sure to pull out the taproot with the rest of the plant. Leaving taproots will cause them to expand, making it more difficult for us to eradicate them in the future. Similarly, when cultivating our internal landscape, it is essential to be thorough and deliberate. At times, large swaths of land must be turned over to make room for new life. In these instances, psychological and emotional taproots may be exposed. As we take the time to study our internal landscape and continue to delve deeper into the layers of Self, we ultimately reach the taproots that have held on the longest. Uprooting these obstructions at their source will yield far greater results than focusing our attention on the many branches that spring forth from a single place of origin.

WEEDS

The word "weeds" often carries with it a negative connotation. They can be thought of as the aspects of self that we desire to be rid of. *However, they are not bad!* A more accurate term might be "undesirables." This reframing fundamentally alters our perception and refines our approach when removing them from our garden. Agronomists have discovered that certain soil conditions are more conducive to particular types of weeds. Therefore, weeds that are present in our internal landscape point us to lessons we must learn about ourselves. They may reveal tendencies or beliefs that govern our day-to-day lives yet hold us back from the self-actualization we seek. Close attention should be paid to the undesirables in our garden. The insight they provide creates the self-awareness that is so invaluable to the process of designing our internal landscape.

EDGE ZONE

Remember, the boundary where two parent ecosystems meet is an edge zone. This place is its own fertile crescent, since the competition for resources makes it a highly productive space. Our internal edge zones are equally fertile.

And we can have an infinite number of them, such as where our values and actions meet, where our emotions and intellect collide, or where past experiences intersect our current behaviors. The opportunity to explore these edge zones is one to be revered, as any cultivation done here stands to produce a yield greater than most other areas. Perhaps your edge zones reveal joy and harmony, or discord and discontent. Regardless, individuals who are consciously committed to awakening their life's core purpose actively seek out these internal edge zones to explore the interdependent spaces that influence their growth and development.

SEASONS OF SELF

In many parts of the world, nature operates on a seasonal cycle where spring turns to summer, then fall, and finally winter. In others, the dry season may turn into the rainy season, then back again. Indeed, we have seasons in our life, as well. Some may be easier to detect than others, and some may last longer than others. Some we may not even recognize as seasons at all, because we have never experienced anything different. Developing an awareness of our internal or social seasons allows for centeredness. Life may be this way or that way right now, but recognizing a new season encourages perspective and patience. Each season's qualities impact us differently. Winter may promote introspection as we slow down and rest, whereas summer might induce excitement and external exploration. The seasons of Self impact us similarly. Perhaps we experience a particular state of being for several weeks, months, or years on end. If we desire that experience to change we may study our internal landscape and make alterations accordingly. Learn to ebb and flow with your seasons of Self. Recognize those you can impact directly, and others you may only experience passively.

ANNUALS

An annual plant grows only for a single season. However, some annuals have adapted to this brief existence by self-seeding, which means they disperse their seed at the end of the season in an attempt to experience life again next year. There are annual plants in our life, as well. Consider the experiences that we "try on for size," only to let them fall away a brief time later. Annuals grow and decay in different seasons of life as we pick up and put down different aspects of ourselves, such as an identity, habit, or acquaintance. When we reflect, we can see how those annual plants have altered our landscapes over the course of time. The timing and nature of those plants are the universe showing us what is needed to align with our life's core purpose. Reflect on your life: what annual habits, beliefs, or behaviors do you possess? Do you enjoy them as annuals, or would you like them to be perennials? Or perhaps they need to be weeded out of your garden altogether?

PERENNIALS

In nature, a perennial plant grows back year after year without needing to reseed. Perennials in our internal landscape are connected to our core identity. In other words, they are the personality traits and characteristics that remain steady and consistent over long periods of time. These attributes undoubtedly shape our identity, and we often perceive them to be rooted in the bedrock of self. It is important to reiterate that every living being is governed by the natural law of life and death. Even perennial plants meet the end of their life. Though these aspects of self have deeply impacted our garden, we are the cultivators of our internal landscape. Therefore, we can decide which aspects of Self we choose to keep as perennials and which we choose to discard. Discarding them does not mean that we ignore or deny them. Rather, it means leaning into them so that we may transform them. We can let go of the long-held narratives that define us. For we are the authors of our own story and the tenders of our own garden.

POLLINATION

Pollination allows nature to spread her seed, and it occurs in different ways. Some plants are abiotic and can self-pollinate. Others are biotic and require another organism to aid in their reproductive process. Humans have the capacity to be both. Of course, we cannot reproduce biologically on our own, but we can pollinate our internal landscape as abiotic creatures. We decide which flowers get our attention, the quality of that attention, and how often it is applied. Our presence in the social and external landscapes allows us to pollinate as biotic creatures. We can pollinate the social landscape with kindness and loving intent, or we can pollinate the external landscape by hand while walking through a garden. It is a matter of self-awareness whether we are pollinating through conscious intent or our intuitive capacities. Regardless, pollination enriches our landscapes and allows them to bear fruit. Whether those fruits are sweet or sour depends on other attributes, such as the health of our soil.

CARBON SEQUESTRATION

Nature has designed her own carbon cycle over time. When the Northern Hemisphere points away from the sun, winter engulfs much of the planet and carbon dioxide builds up in Earth's atmosphere. When the Northern Hemisphere points toward the sun, that seasonal effect reverses, and excess carbon dioxide is sequestered in vegetation. As individuals, we all have our own atmosphere in the form of our energetic field, and it is possible for "greenhouse gases" to build up in that field. This can happen through undesirable forms of habitual thought, emotions, or energetic patterns. Once these unwanted energies reach certain levels, they negatively impact our internal ecology. At this point, we can begin to engage in drawdown. Soil is the largest land-based carbon sink, and it is possible to design the soil of our internal landscape to sequester unwanted energies. By drawing down undesirable aspects from our energetic field, we can return them to the soils of Self for composting and increase our fertility. The beauty is that carbon is an essential building block of life. Once we figure out how to achieve drawdown, we increase the capacity of life and vitality within ourselves and our surroundings.

LEARN
WITH NATURE

All of the answers lie before us. They are quite literally underneath our feet, inside our minds, and within our hearts. As Bill Mollison, the founder of permaculture, once said, "Though the problems of the world are increasingly complex, the solutions remain embarrassingly simple." If we desire to restore balance between humans and the natural world—to reverse climate collapse and restore Earth to the garden of Eden that is her natural state—we must reconnect ourselves to the environment around us and within us. Though it may not be easy, it can be simple. The Earth's only request, our only responsibility, is to honor our relationship with the natural world. To redesign our collective dance with the Earth and remember that we long to experience her bounty. She remains the eternal womb, willing to receive us with the grace and acceptance she holds for all beings.

Nature must become our teacher once again, and we must embrace humility and demonstrate a willingness to live humbly amongst all beings on Earth. Our attempt to conquer the natural world has resulted in our severance from it, and this dichotomy perpetuates an unsustainable existence. We do not need more technical fixes; we require adaptive solutions. This adaptive process will turn over entire industries and cultures, but to achieve it, individuals must redesign their relationship with themselves and one another. Doing so will restructure society and revive humanity along the way. These challenges are merely opportunities in disguise, and they call forth solutions so simple and plain to see that we literally walk among them every day.

We must only reclaim ourselves to bring about this reality. Of course, this is not permission to be self-absorbed or self-centered; these attributes have contributed to the social upheaval and climate catastrophes of our time. Instead, it is *revival* that we are after. *Saving yourself is the greatest gift you can give the Earth and humanity.* "Selfishly" pursuing your own liberation will invoke the selflessness required to restore the commons. We must rediscover the nature of our true Self. In doing so, we allow ourselves to be guided by an inner knowing of an

outer truth: we are all one, interconnected by the energetic ties we share with Mother Earth and the strands
that tie her, in turn, to the cosmos.

SPIRITUAL LANDSCAPE

DEFINING THE
SPIRITUAL LANDSCAPE

The fabric that connects the internal, social, and external landscapes is often unseen and unspoken. It is this *space between* that acts as the omnipotent and omnipresent energy of life itself. It is present in all beings all the time, everywhere. Taoists refer to it as the Tao itself: "here before the beginning of beginningless time," as Lao Tzu states in the *Tao Te Ching*. Of course, Lao Tzu also suggests, "The Tao that can be named is not the true Tao." So read this final section through *sensation*. Take these words with a grain of salt, because your experience of the spiritual landscape is unique and transcends the intellectual, emotional, and energetic impact contained in this book.

Believing that our five senses tell us all we need to know about the world distances us from the true nature of life itself. Was it pure intellect that brought Einstein to his theory of relativity? Certainly it was not. Einstein himself expressed the importance of wonder and exploration, our intuitive capacities, and the mystery of God. One cannot teach what can only be learned. And one cannot give what can only be earned. So, while there is no way to explain the spiritual landscape, an attempt shall nonetheless be made. How else can we make sense of the moment when we look out across the landscape and feel overtaken by gratitude for its beauty? How else can we comprehend the synchronicity of life when we stumble upon the solution to a challenge we did not know we had? How else can we describe the moments when we are overwhelmed by joy and ecstasy for no apparent reason? These are indeed spiritual experiences, for life itself is an exercise in spiritual exploration.

INEFFABLE

The spiritual landscape is ineffable, too great to be described in words. Trying to classify the spiritual landscape would be like trying to classify every organism on planet Earth—a futile exercise. Not only is the landscape itself infinite, but it is ever-evolving. The creative capacities of the cosmos outweigh any human's perceptive abilities by a significant margin. Choosing not to acknowledge the spiritual landscape means shutting off your ability to perceive the macrocosm. Like an iceberg, the vastness of the cosmos cannot be perceived through conscious thought. To access the great beyond, we must be literate in the language of body consciousness.

Clairvoyance, clairsentience, clairaudience, telepathy, and other intuitive abilities are fundamental expressions of a soul that has access to universal truths that lie "below the surface," or beyond three-dimensional sensing. Though words can attempt to describe these experiences, they will invariably fall short. This does not mean the spiritual landscape lacks objective truths. Indeed, there are many truths that can be confirmed by those who are able to pierce the veil and access insight from beyond the third dimension. Humans can access the twelfth dimension and beyond. We must look to the greater beyond for new ways to bridge worlds. There is a network of support in place to protect new worlds that are emerging onto the universal field; humans are not alone.

Many of us have accepted the belief that because we are so small, and the spiritual landscape so vast, we cannot have any significant impact on it. How wrong we would be! Consider the intricately woven nature of the natural world. Recognize that the Earth is stitched to the fabric of the cosmos the same way we have been threaded to her. Just like ripples from a stone dropped in a pond, any thought, decision, or action ripples outward into the ether that knows no bounds. We possess an innate capacity to interact with the cosmos through vibration and energetic frequency. These frequencies are the objective realities that can be realized when a greater number of the population cultivates themselves. Understanding those frequencies is just like learning a second language. It takes time, commitment, and guidance to become literate in the energies that flow through us. The part we play as individuals is just one drop in a sea of drops; yet together, we fill an ocean.

When we understand how our energy impacts the landscapes around us, we recognize the profound impact we have in the world. The spiritual landscape is an intelligent canvas that allows us to collaborate energetically. This possibility to paint a more beautiful picture of the cosmos is an indescribable opportunity. If our inner energies align appropriately, we can perceive the greater beyond. This understanding allows us to be teacher and student simultaneously as our actions become guided by powers beyond our biological existence. We become faithful and trustworthy shepherds of ancient wisdom. At the same time, we remain receptive novices regarding all the inner workings of the universe. This allows us to cultivate a healthy balance of doing and undoing, being and nonbeing, seeing and unseeing. Ultimately, it allows us to lead from behind, and to understand the outer world by exploring the inner world.

BEING OF SERVICE

Seeking to satiate our base instincts, we become stuck in an energetic rut. This cycle attracts similar experiences and vibrations, reinforcing a lower frequency. Without self-awareness and regulation, it can be exceedingly difficult to escape the cycle. Attempting to satiate the insatiable is part of the human condition. But spiritual ascension requires that we continually hold ourselves accountable to a life of service. Living a life of service allows us to keep our intentions pure and unsullied. This common phrase holds true: with great power comes great responsibility.

The great beyond and biological life share the same drive: to seek balance. The same can be said of our inner ecology. The body acts as a tuning fork, enabling us to perceive the subtle differences that distinguish light from dark. The channels that open and allow us to perceive the divine are the same channels through which darkness speaks. Therefore, it is imperative that we continually revisit body consciousness as it confirms or denies virtuous action and intent. After all, a life not lived in service of others is not a spiritual life. Simultaneously, a life not lived in service of Self is no spiritual life at all. It is the ultimate expression of harmony to live in service. Our lives become one great balancing act, like an ecosystem perpetually engineering new ways to rise above the challenges that seek to snuff out consciousness while also embracing the winding journey of life.

The sunflower turns its head to follow the sun across the sky, and we do not need to understand the inner workings of the plant to appreciate its magnificence. There is deep purpose and simultaneously great beauty, and that is enough. The same is true for our existence on this planet. We do not need to be able to explain and classify every experience or instinct; we must only understand ourselves *well enough*. To accept a life of service means embracing our greater calling while staying grounded with the taproots of humility and curiosity.

Imagine a world filled with beings seeking to bring about unity. How does that *feel*? We must only devote *ourselves* to living a life of service to bring that world about. Remember, we do not need to activate the masses; we must only reach critical mass. It is then that the human species will spill over the tipping point of conscious evolution just as water rushes over the falls in front of it. Instead of leaving behind a wake of destruction, lovingkindness and acceptance will be the imprint of our footsteps. If the harmonious world described above seems fictitious and out of reach, trust that it is entirely possible so long as we each do our own deep internal work.

DEEP WORK

For those of us not yet aware of our intuitive abilities, know that they can be accessed through disciplined training and deep internal work. Nature's law of balance suggests that to ascend to the highest heights, we must also descend to the deepest depths. There is no escaping this reality. Nor is there a detour around the deep and often difficult internal work. Yet the soul inherently recognizes these challenges and yearns to commit to them. It is in those challenges that we sense the true power of living a life worth breathing, and from then on, the only thing capable of satisfying the soul is the breath of life itself.

By making the conscious commitment to design your inner landscape and seek your true north, you have already begun to awaken your life's core purpose. In the beginning, our core purpose *is* to discover our core purpose. As we engage in the deep work that accompanies this process, we uncover personal insights that enable us to advance the evolution of human consciousness. Committing to this inner work and showing up as our best self inspires others and grabs the attention of greater powers. Balance is restored as we become conscious of life's unimaginable gifts. For how do we know the touch of hot if we do not know cold? How do we know the divine if we do not know deceit? How can we embody the spirit of boldness if we do not know meekness? If we desire to experience the wholeness of life, we must embrace all it has to offer.

Living a life connected to our core purpose requires deep work. The great irony of this path is that the deep work requires no effort in and of itself. Effort comes from the way we define the process, but the process itself is neutral and natural. The caterpillar does not shy away from becoming a butterfly. It commits to its own process of transformation with a natural disposition. It does not need to understand the life that awaits after the cocoon; it must only accept and commit to its journey. No matter where we are in our life's cycle, a simple commitment to the deep work that lies ahead is all we need to enter our next phase. When we do this, something is revealed that the Creator herself is excited to witness. It is then, and only then, that we leave the cocoon behind. No butterfly has the same markings, no ladybug has the same spots, no fish has the same scales, and no bird has the same feathers. Spend the time, commit to yourself, and let your full plumage be on display for others.

BUMPER RAILS OF THE
SPIRITUAL PATH

Essential and subjective insights are revealed during the deep work of Self. However, there are objective truths embedded in spiritual teachings throughout time. At times, walking this path of awakening is analogous to bowling. We are all playing the same game; we each have our own lane; and we all share the same objective, which is to knock down as many pins of spiritual development as possible. Spiritual texts, religions, and faith-based philosophies provide us with bumper rails for the spiritual path and landscape. They are designed to keep us traveling toward our destination (which, not by accident, comes from the root word "destiny"). A brief study of spiritual philosophies reveals a great deal about the spiritual landscape.

As we embark on a very brief, high-level overview of some of the world's largest faith-based practices, we can see similarities emerge. Let this reinforce the truth that no matter our spiritual or religious orientation, personal beliefs, or the path we walk toward awakening, as a collective, we share a single unified intent. As such, we can illuminate the threshold where our spiritual work transitions from the subjective to the objective, both personally and collectively.

But before we move to the objective, I must first disclose the subjective. Please note that I write from the social conditioning of a white, cisgendered, heterosexual, American male. As such, I have interviewed others who identify with the particular faiths represented in the table below in an attempt to acknowledge and address my subjectivity. This endeavor is not meant to be an exhaustive exploration of the world's major faith philosophies. Rather, it is meant to spark critical contemplation and provocative exploration. Indeed, the most appropriate way to seek God, enlightenment, nirvana, or liberation is always up for interpretation.

Therefore, with the caveat that this exercise is an inevitable oversimplification, I will categorize below the many different faith variations under a single spiritual umbrella and distill all teachings to their most basic form. Some fields are left blank because that faith-philosophy either may not have any direct teachings related to that concept, espouse that it does not exist, or simply be too complex to summarize effectively.

Faith-Based Similarities & Simplification

	Indigenous American Spirituality	Hinduism	Taoism	Buddhism	Islam	Judaism	Christianity
Creator	Great Spirit (or Great Mystery)	Brahman	The Tao		Allah	Adonai (or Elohim)	God
Spiritual Path	Red Road	Grihastha Sannyasa	Tao	The Middle Way	Sunnah The Straight Path	Halakha	Discipleship Follow God through Christ
Spiritual Realms	Sky Earth Underworld	Heaven Earth Underworld	Heaven Earth Man	Gods Demi-Gods Humans Animals Hungry Ghosts Hell	The First Determination The Second Determination Noetic Realm Imaginal Realm Material Realm	Heaven Earth Emanation Creation Formation Action	Heaven Earth Hell Purgatory
Guiding Principles	Seven Sacred Virtues or Teachings Animism Harmony with Nature	Dharma Samsara Karma Moksha	Wu wei Yin and Yang Harmony with Nature	Three Marks of Existence The Four Noble Truths The Eightfold Path Karma	Five Pillars Sharia Law	Ten Commandments 613 Mitzvot Tikkun Olam	Ten Commandments The Beatitudes
Universal Energy		Prana	Qi	Prana			Holy Spirit
Be Aware of	All Life is Sacred and Interrelated	Yamas Niyamas	Six Greedy Thieves Seven Bloodthirsty Devils	Five Precepts Five Hindrances	Halal Haram	Yetzer Hara Seven Laws of Noah	Sin Justice

Even though the world's largest faith-based philosophies are wildly diverse, we can still see patterns begin to emerge. For example, all put forth a template for guidance; many promote a state of inner clarity, self-management, and righteous intent. Each of these spiritual philosophies provides its own template for how to move in and through any landscape. Each puts forth the notion of living a spiritually guided life. And most promote an awareness that warns of potential hindrances on our spiritual journey.

As spiritual novices, we need these bumper rails, to return to the original analogy. Naturally, as we grow and develop, we have the desire to bowl without them, but if we have not learned how to consistently stay on the path without the need of the bumper rails, we slip off the lane and into the gutter. Once stuck in that rut, it can be difficult to escape. Often, life in the gutter is simply our attempt to fulfill ego desires through whatever neurosis we prefer that day. The spiritual path itself becomes less and less appealing, until we reach a point when our suffering is so great that we must turn and face it. Many in the recovery community report a rock-bottom moment that was their impetus for change. Collectively, as a species, we are now at our rock-bottom moment. Human life cannot sustain itself much longer with our current consumptive habits. Yet, just like bowling, when we fall in the gutter, life gives us another ball to roll.

The art of spiritual development is the essential practice of staying on the path. It does not matter what lane we are in, what faith we follow, or if we follow a faith at all. What matters is that we recognize our commonality. Spiritual teachings act as a rudder for the ship we sail day and night. Why does the monk stay on the mountain and live an austere life? In part, because limiting distractions creates space for attunement. This is not to suggest that we must all find our way to the mountain top. Rather, it is an opportunity to pause and reflect. What areas of your life are not aligned with your highest Self and purpose? What do your distractions and temptations teach you about your spiritual development? How will you hold yourself accountable to staying on the path and keep your bowling ball rolling toward the pins of virtue?

These "bumper rails" of guidance are not punitive. Indeed, they are there to support our journey toward a righteous existence free of conditioning. By saying no to distractions, we amplify our ability to say yes to what matters most. We design our landscapes in such a way that allows our soul to flourish. We cultivate a lifestyle that enables us to touch the innermost aspect of Self for the sake of spiritual awakening.

If the analogy of bowling is not helpful, we might think of walking the spiritual path as a plane ascending from the runway at takeoff. It requires a tremendous amount of energy just to get the plane moving, slowly we gain traction, and eventually we achieve liftoff. Once off the ground, we have a bit more latitude than before. Now we are not committed to the straight and narrow path of the runway, but we still need conscious commitment to reach cruising altitude, so we keep full speed ahead. Eventually, we break through the clouds, and everything becomes clear. Clarity is a consequence of our efforts during takeoff and ascension.

If you have not already, find your runway or lane. Set boundaries and put up the bumper rails if you need to. Consider, through self-study, what is required to hold you accountable to walking your path. For every one of us, there is a turning point, a final moment when we can still choose, consciously or unconsciously, whether or not to fall into the gutter. This is not to suggest that one day we will live a perfect life. Rather, there comes a point where we have traveled far enough that we are bound to knock over some pins. Our goal is to find ways to manage ourselves to that point and beyond. Of course, we must also remember that the spiritual path rarely unfolds in a linear way. Letting go of this expectation helps us embrace the turbulence—the back and forth—while clearing the way toward a virtuous life.

DAILY SADHANA

By developing a daily sadhana, or practice, we create a structure to simplify our spiritual endeavors. A daily sadhana is
a means of simplifying the process of awakening through
consistent spiritual practices. It becomes a tether we orient
to and from. A truly awakened soul will not require such a
routine, but you and I should not consider ourselves so for-
tunate. It is through this discipline that we realize Self and
awaken our life's core purpose more fully.

A daily sadhana can include anything that brings you
into conscious awareness. Perhaps you start your day with
time devoted to silence in the form of meditation and energy
arts. Or you access the divine through exercise or endurance
training. Or maybe your sadhana includes reading spiritual
scripture or chanting. No matter the structure, remember
the law of balance. A sadhana is meant to attune the mind,
body, and heart to the spirit that is always connected. What
matters is to what extent that connection is known and felt

consciously. This consistency in our daily practice begins to iron out the inconsistencies of life's irregularities. We bring forth a structure that helps us move from where we are to exactly where we are meant to be.

Intuition is always speaking, but are you always listening? Is your lifestyle conducive to hearing your inner voice and aligning your actions with your highest purpose? The ability to do God's work dwindles with distance as one drifts away from spirit. Develop a daily sadhana and watch your world evolve into a single practice that reflects your devotion to the divine. Remaining diligent in your efforts creates a consistency that inspires the desire to ground so that your spirit can subsequently launch.

Routine builds consistency and consistency builds trust— trust of Self. Do you trust yourself wholly and completely? Regardless of your answer, consider implementing a daily sadhana and begin that journey toward inner trust, self-worth, and ascension.

LIVING A
GUIDED LIFE

Once we have uncovered our true north and made the conscious commitment to awaken our life's core purpose, *the act of living becomes the art of listening.* Awareness, body consciousness, and self-reflection create the capacity to live life in accordance with a higher purpose. To do this, we must be able to access wisdom from the guides and guideposts in our lives. Every individual has at least one spiritual guide who aids us in this lifetime. Though it is helpful to be able to hear and converse with these guides, that level of intuition generally requires an immense amount of self-cultivation. It should also be noted that this relationship is absolutely unnecessary to live a guided life. As an alternative, we can become adept at reading the body's signs and signals, as intuition so often speaks through body consciousness. A clear, calm, and consciously aware mind and body make this easier.

Though the universe can speak with blunt force, her more regular method of communication is a quiet whisper and gentle nudge. Living a guided life requires the desire and capacity to *tune in* to the frequencies of the cosmos. A spiritually guided life is not always the bed of rose petals it is made out to be in popular culture. And the desire to stay engaged is essential for when the going gets tough. Those who have cultivated themselves sufficiently can share stories of the darkness they have encountered on their path. It is simply the nature of balance expressing itself. The more light one shines, the more darkness will come to snuff it out. However, for those still traveling their path, each will say it has been entirely worth it. The soul desires to be forged in the fires of adversity. It is in those moments that we encounter our core and develop our integrity. The opportunity to become a lighthouse amidst the often dark and murky waters of life is one to be revered.

Once we know our ship inside and out, we become proficient at navigating the choppy waters of life. We become so familiar with our internal landscape that we can access a calm contentment at any given time and in any given circumstance. Our spiritual journey is not necessarily a tale of two halves, but along the way, we will come to know the light and love that all awakened beings speak of. Resilience and gratitude become cornerstones of our existence, and joyful abundance is a consequence of life as our desires dissipate.

Living a guided life is a matter of free will. Though fate most certainly exists, we all can continue living a life more mundane than necessary. But for those of us who recognize the opportunity humanity faces at this time, we see the necessity of this path and practice in our lives. We recognize that we are making a conscious commitment to live a guided life—a life that will often be accompanied by spiritual powers beyond our comprehension and awareness. A life that encourages us to explore the unknown areas of our internal and spiritual landscapes. A life that inspires others to do the same.

MINIMALISM &
SIMPLICITY

Minimalism and simplicity are necessary tools in a guided life. Limiting distractions can be useful when attuning our minds and bodies to the frequencies necessary for guidance. As we explore our internal landscape, we must eliminate external distractions. We must clear the brush so that we can expose the soil underneath. Minimalism and simplicity allow us to do so. The awakened soul knows that it requires very little for survival and satiation. It also understands that distractions throw us out of balance, and it responds by pulling us back to center.

The desire to pursue the next shiny object may never fully disappear in this lifetime. However, once we awaken awareness, we realize that these shiny objects are unnecessary for our spiritual maturation. At that time, they begin to lose their luster. Once we have polished the mirror of self and can see our reflection clearly, distractions come into focus. Of course, all of life's experiences are simply signs and guideposts on our path. We do not need to label them, judge them, or even go looking for them; we simply acknowledge their presence and thank them for their guidance. A truly attuned mind does not perceive the world through a binary perspective, as this strips the spiritual essence from life itself. Instead, they see balance, and this draws them deeper into communion with the cosmos. When we miss the forest for the trees, we become unable or unwilling to see deeper meaning in life's experiences. To live a guided life and move purposefully toward our true north, we understand that a balanced disposition is essential.

Minimalism and simplicity do not require us to withhold pleasure from our lives; they are not limiting. Instead, they empower us to be limitless. The Buddha taught us that our attachments bring us pain. Attachments keep us tethered to a physical world and our psychological drama. They keep us from ascending to the spiritual landscape that receives us the same way a loving mother receives her child, with simplicity and elegance.

The cornerstones of minimalism and simplicity release us from the belief that fulfilling our desires will bring freedom. Remember, true freedom is being free from desires. *Letting go is the path to receiving life's greatest bounty. Opening up is the path to closing off our insecurities. Sitting still is the path to spiritual progress.* If you find yourself longing for life to be this way or that, do not get discouraged! Instead, practice gratitude for what you have and embrace the opportunity to turn your desires into fertile compost for the seeds you are meant to sow.

KNOW SELF,
NO SELF

One of the great challenges in life is to be born a unique entity with the singular task of rediscovering our connectedness to the spiritual landscape. Our own mind erects the boundaries that we believe separate us from one another and the world. To recognize that we are almost entirely empty space—electrons rotating around central nuclei, exchanging particles with the world around us—shatters the conceptual reality of an individual self. The only thing that separates us is the idea of separation itself.

The Buddhist notion that there is no self is contradictory to most Western values and beliefs. Many of us have been so conditioned into the notion of self that nonself is difficult to even fathom. Certainly, this makes it difficult to leap from this truth-of-self to the dissolution of self altogether. However, it is possible and has been done an untold number of times by countless "individuals" throughout the course of history.

Life presents us with the opportunity to recognize its subtle nature time and again. For the intellectual who believes they have mastered minimalism and simplicity, to learn there is more to life than thinking. For the emotive being who seeks only pleasure, to recognize that a bit of emotional pain can be part of a life well lived. For the clairvoyant who enjoys surfing the cosmic waves, to see that maximizing their impact in this world means connecting with this world. And for the teacher who senses how to guide devotees down the path, to recognize they are not the cause of a student's progress.

The paradox of life is that only a sufficiently cultivated Self can see there is no self. Humans need not renounce all the insight and innovation we have come to know over the millennia. Instead, we are called to transcend that knowledge and enter a space where we put the Earth and others before ourselves. The more we know our true nature, the less we need. The less we need, the more we have to give. The more we have to give, the more we benefit the landscapes around us. In the end, we see that this lifetime is not about us at all. It is simply an opportunity to serve. Realizing this allows us to focus on cultivating what matters most—our souls.

It is no mystery that material possessions cannot be taken with us into the afterlife. What we take with us is our inner cultivation and karma. To *know* Self is to allow for the emergence of *no-self*. No-self allows us to deconstruct the barriers we have erected in an attempt to keep us safe. Allow your *self* to melt away into the fabric of the spiritual landscape. Let the cosmic flow express itself through you, so that others may bear witness and build a bridge to their own spiritually guided life.

TAKING RISKS IS A
MATTER OF FAITH

Building a bridge over often troubled waters requires risk, and faith is the underbelly of risk. Undoubtedly, you have sensed that risk is inevitable when pursuing your true north and awakening your life's core purpose. This is healthy and meant to be embraced as it helps you develop self-assurance. Every living being has this in common: The leaf takes a risk when it lets go of the tree. The Earth takes a risk fostering life in the vacuum of space. Any mammal takes a risk when it leaves its mother for the first time. Faithfully committing to the unknown is conscious commitment, the backbone of any decision on the path of self-cultivation. *Faith is the fascia and tissue that bind us to the spiritual landscape.*

Trust and faith are invariably intertwined. To awaken ourselves and align with our highest calling, we have to trust the process. To hold faith that the great unknown will receive us is the same faith that a newborn child displays when it leaves the world of a mother's womb. It is our responsibility to stitch the quilt of society in such a way that encourages others to take leaps of faith. We do not know if the safety net is secure until we test it. But to find out, we must face our fear and take the risk.

No matter the person or circumstance, taking risks induces fear. Biologically, we are hardwired to avoid fear and, therefore, risk. We have learned over the course of evolution that risk and fear are often associated with death. Yet, death itself is not something to fear. It simply marks the ultimate process of transformation. A yin answer to a yang life. Between now and then, taking risks may result in so-called "mini-deaths"— the death and decay of old habits or beliefs, the severance of emotional ties or relationships, and the end of self-doubt or self-limiting beliefs. Allow yourself to embrace risk-taking. Develop a sense of faith that the world will receive you and, more importantly, develop a sense of self-trust. Trust that, with or without a safety net, you will receive yourself.

This is why the cultivation of a healthy internal landscape is so essential for wellbeing. To go boldly into the unknown, to forge ahead with nothing but an internal fire to guide us—on the surface, it appears terrifying, but underneath, we revel in the exhilaration. After we leap and before we reach the safety net, the soul is alive. As we jump into the unknown time and again, we trust in our training and increase our risk tolerance, enabling us to take ever greater leaps of faith.

HEART CONSCIOUSNESS

Before we begin with our exploration of heart consciousness, let us first paint a picture of the heart through a bit of scientific research. Science has demonstrated that the magnetic field of the heart is substantially larger than that of the brain. It can be measured several feet beyond the surface of the body. In the energy-art practice of qigong, Wei Qi is a protective layer of Qi that extends beyond the body. Because Qi is bioelectromagnetic energy, we might consider the heart to be of the same substance, biologically based and carrying an electric as well as magnetic charge. Taking this into account, is the existence of Qi really all that difficult to accept?

Heart consciousness is the ability to fuse our bioelectromagnetic energy field with our spiritual consciousness. It allows us to literally connect Heaven and Earth, ignite any torch, and shine light in any dark place. To access heart consciousness, one must set a pure and virtuous intention. There is no place for impurities within the realm of heart consciousness. It *is* the white light that spiritually inclined members of our society often speak of. It elevates the human vessel beyond this dimension and connects us with higher realms that guide our greater calling. As you might suspect, conjuring this energy requires a deep level of awareness and cultivation.

Has there ever been a time in your life that you could literally feel your heart swell? Perhaps it may have been an emotional response to a pleasant experience or an insightful realization following deep contemplation? In essence, this is how the heart is meant to communicate. As we access this energy, we invoke lovingkindness. The light of our consciousness shines through the darkness and heals ourselves, others, and the Earth. We are wholesome beings meant to live wholesome lives. The ability to access heart consciousness aligns our true nature and our highest purpose.

Every person has the ability to access heart consciousness. However, those willing to cultivate themselves deeply are most likely to experience it to the fullest extent. With every new risk taken, we strengthen our faith, as well as the spiritual landscape. This allows us to access deeper levels of inner cultivation, which in turn results in higher levels of awareness. This is simply the nature of balance expressing itself in our lives. We become consciously aware of our inner landscape's connectedness to the spiritual landscape. When this happens, our self-imposed separation dissolves and we are left exposed, receptive, and flexible. Emotional vulnerability allows us to experience greater depths of the human experience. It paves a path toward heart consciousness and an evolved collective conscience.

LOVE

This is the answer. It is so simple and yet so profound—love is the path of least resistance and the path of most disruption. It is the true way. To live through love allows us to decompose the conceptual barriers that distance us from the world and to strengthen our connection to life itself. If we are the needle and life is the fabric, love is the thread that sews us together.

Nature expresses love in an infinite number of ways. The mother makes space for her young in the nest. The emperor penguin warms the egg throughout an entire arctic winter. The salmon swims upstream to spawn. The mother elephant plays with her young. The mason bee exchanges pollen for nectar. The tendril of the vining plant gently wraps around its host. Fungi exchange nutrients between plants and the soil. Love is simply symbiosis, and the Earth has perfected this art.

Is there competition in nature? Of course. But cohesion and balance are always on display in ecological systems. It is our highest calling as a species to revive this love and cultivate it within ourselves, to rekindle an ecological rever-ence that abides by the principles of balance and cohesion. Love has allowed us to co-evolve with nature over the course of human history, and it will guide us as we embark on the journey of our next chapter in human evolution.

NATURE'S
FREQUENCY

We do not need to look to the future to determine whether our current existence is sustainable. We must move away from the belief that humans have the right to take what we desire from others or the Earth. We must recognize our obligation to care for ourselves, others, and the land. Indigenous cultures across the globe have embodied this for millennia. Eco-reverence has guided their actions and beliefs, societies and cultures, as well as their hearts and souls. The answers we seek are before us and all around us. It is our time to lift up this awareness and unite all of humanity under this single, shared truth. *This process starts with you.*

The Earth is indeed fully capable of taking care of herself; this is not in question. What is in question is whether we will choose to stay and learn, once again; to cooperate; to be part of the flock, not the self-appointed shepherd; and to embrace this infinite landscape that she has set before us. She existed before we arrived and will exist long after we are gone. She is the ultimate Giving Tree. To *believe* that the Earth's purpose is to enable human indulgence is to separate ourselves from the sentient nature of her existence. What if the Earth herself desires to experience the freezing and thawing of the ice caps each season? What if she desires to breathe fresh air in her atmosphere and drink clean water in her rivers? What if she desires to see the fish swim in the ocean and the animals of the great plains roam freely? Let us *all* restore our capacity to live, love, and learn to co-create with Mother Earth once again.

NATURE IS
YOUR SPIRIT

Extreme heat powers the Earth's core, and the human heart could be comparably viewed as the core of a human. Earth resonates at 7.83 hertz and the human heart resonates at a frequency of 1.0 hertz. Your life's *core* purpose resonates at a specific frequency as well. You must find that frequency and let it be expressed in all you do. Our great quest in life is to strip away the layers of distraction until we can sit peacefully at our center, discover our true nature, awaken our life's core purpose, and find the frequency that will resonate in harmony with the world around us. This process can only happen naturally and must be guided by an inner knowing. All the self-help theories in the world will not measure up to the tiniest sliver of honest self-study.

If we fail to awaken to the soil of our spirit, then we must work feverishly and perhaps in futility to escape the sixth mass extinction. If we cling to our current consumptive paradigm, we will resist change, because it will feel as though we are clamping down on our freedoms. Without our awakening, it will require great effort to reform everything from industry and policy to family and individuality. However, if we reclaim ourselves and revive our innermost truth, we will transform humanity one spirit at a time. The simple nature of life will reveal itself to the masses, and we will be drawn inward, mesmerized, like watching a fire at night or waves gently lapping upon the shore. We will recognize that more is, in fact, less. We will set down our desires for overconsumption the same way an addict sets down the bottle for the last time. We will understand inherently that our single purpose in life is to find the frequency of our soul and resonate in harmony with nature.

We have a choice. We can go down kicking and screaming, or allow our souls to ascend as we dig into the soil of spirit. We can surf the cosmic waves of life like a dolphin who playfully bounds in the water, or glide along the airstream of consciousness like the great eagle soaring above. Though we are of this world, we are not bound by it. Though we may suffer now, we need not. Though we may have lost hope, there is always a path forward. The choice is ours. The choice is yours.

SUMMARY

My sincerest hope is that this book provided insight and spiritual sustenance, pointing you toward wonder, curiosity, and excitement; engaging you in self-reflection and self-study; and reviving a conscious commitment to your awakening as you walk the path less traveled.

For there is a difference between being awake and getting out of bed. To speak of a life well-lived does not automatically equate to living that life. My wish is for you to search your community and find an accountability buddy on your spiritual journey. Think and feel carefully about whom you select, as you must share with them what is on your mind and in your heart. Indeed, we must all do this internal work in solitude, but it must also be done in community. Remember: saving ourselves is the greatest gift we can give the world. This process will not unfold until we relax into it and take big risks with the faith that the bosom of the Earth and all of Creation will receive us. As we engage in our own deep work, we will inspire others to do the same. The unfolding of this process will bring us to critical mass.

First, spend time getting to know *your* nature. To learn your nature, spend time in nature. Some of us love to dream and ideate, while others cringe at creative visioning. For the dreamers, let the feeling tone of life guide you in the direction of your true north. For the feelers, let body awareness and consciousness commitment guide you to your core purpose. Whether you are energized by the process of deep reflection or prefer to just watch everything unfold, *do that!* What you dream up intellectually is almost assuredly not your life's core purpose. So, pay attention to the feedback the cosmos provides and allow yourself to be guided toward a more virtuous life. Either way, commit to the practice of taking risks.

Your first risk could be a one hundred-day gong. The word "gong" translates roughly to "practice," and in some Eastern philosophies, one hundred-day gongs are associated with traditional methods of self-cultivation. Commit to something for one hundred days, and if you miss a day, you must start over from zero. It is an excellent means of habit building *if* we can hold ourselves accountable. Perhaps your gong is one hundred days of self-reflection and self-study, or physical fitness, or a mindfulness practice, or writing that book that has been brewing inside you for years. No matter what it is, commit to it. It is conscious commitment and disciplined follow-through that will save us all.

Some of us must first learn to manage ourselves well before we understand our higher purpose. Others might know the direction of their true north and struggle to take the leap. Neither path is more or less virtuous, and neither person is more or less worthy. Both must engage in the deep work of self-actualization. It is discipline, coupled with a clear purpose, that creates the conditions required to touch the true nature of our spirit. We cannot escape the experience of life. We are bound to it the same way an insect is bound to a spider's web. Therefore, we must not only accept but embrace the truths that are presented to us. *Change is the only constant, and the only way out is in and through that change.* Learn to feel when you are compromising Self, and respond accordingly. We overcome by becoming, not by overpowering. Yield to life and feel for the path as it unfolds underfoot.

Joseph Campbell once said, "The cave you fear to enter holds the treasure you seek." There is no shame in feeling pain, doubt, or fear. Indeed, these emotions are to be embraced! Leaning into emotional vulnerability, turning to face the shadows that reside within is the only way to shine light on those areas. Otherwise, they remain in darkness, and we remain governed by our inability to see beyond them.

So, go forth—be bold and always remember that there is only one time to truly live. That time is right now. Whether you discover or design your life's core purpose, pursuing the path is what matters most.

CONCLUSION

With increasing rates of infertility, chronic disease, soil degradation, and climate collapse, the survival of homo sapiens
has become increasingly precarious. Scientists predict that
by 2045 we will be producing 40 percent less food and have
a global population north of nine billion. In 2017, theoretical
physicist Stephen Hawking suggested humans need to find
another planet to colonize within one hundred years or we
will face extinction. It has been suggested that Einstein once
said humans would have only a few years left to survive if
bees were to disappear from the face of the Earth. A grim
outlook for human existence indeed.

This is not the fate we desire for our children. The salva-
tion of our species and all manifestations of biological life
require us to course-correct. We must come to terms with
our hubris and turn toward our divinity. Our separation from

nature has brought nothing but destruction. Our attempts to exist outside the bounds of natural law are futile. The human race inhabits planet Earth within a solar system and a galaxy that, in turn, exists in infinite space. Our true nature is infinite. We are simply the coagulation of stardust, imbued with a wisdom and intelligence that can only be described as divine.

Our responsibility is to save ourselves and revive humanity, to restore the soil, sea, and sky, one landscape at a time. As we begin to stitch ourselves back together, we become the sewing needle guided by the fingers of God. We become a tool for the evolution of consciousness in the form of authentic embodiment, an existence rooted in simplicity and patience, an integrity fueled by humility, compassion, and curiosity. We are left with no other option but to embrace the aquifers of ancient wisdom that reside within all of us.

This process is the undercurrent that guides the evolutionary journey of coexistence and cooperation. It teaches us how to listen, how to see, and how to sense beyond any boundaries imposed on us by self or society. We may all touch the ancient love that makes life itself possible with conscious awareness. We need only turn toward it and embrace the soil of our spirit. Life is always worth living, and we must connect Heaven and Earth through the sentience of our own soul.

This journey is unending. Let us always remember that whatever we do not awaken in this lifetime will be waiting for us in the next. It may not be easy, but it can be simple.

All my love and sincerest support to you.

Live to Learn,

Learn to Love,

Love to Live,

Ian C. Williams

ACKNOWLEDGMENTS

As with all creations, this book would not exist without the support of so many. From the seeds of purpose sown long ago, to the deep work and transformational change that continues to guide my path, my gratitude is unparalleled. First and foremost, thank you, the reader. This book is fundamentally, at its core, an act of service. Without you, these pontifications would remain reverberations in between my ears and documents in my hard drive that would never see the light of day. Thank you for taking a leap of faith and devoting your time and energy to exploring what this book has to offer. I pray that it has provided something of value on your journey.

To my loving wife, endearing friend, and partner in life, Julie. Thank you for demonstrating day in and day out the grace of unconditional love. You provide a soft space to come home to each night, and a solid platform to launch from each morning. Without your patience and support, this book would not have been written. To my parents, Kris and Keith, and my sister, Anya. Thank you for all the love, nurturing intent, and space to roam freely throughout my youth. I hope by now, your cortisol levels have returned to more normal levels, and I thank you for receiving me with open arms and warm hearts. Words truly cannot express the perfection of our union; I am entirely honored to call you family. And to Trina, Tyler, and Kristen. Though I do not claim to know the purpose of your respective passings, I know the processes your departures have sparked in my life. Thank you for reminding me each day that life is a privilege, not a right. Your influence is forever etched in my heart and at the core of this message.

To the entire Scribe Media team. Particularly, Eliece Pool for your publishing manager expertise, Liz Diresbach for your patience and responsiveness throughout the cover design process, Erik van Mechelen for the courageous conversations regarding book title, and Annaliese Hoehling for your guidance through QA. To Brannan Sirratt, editor extraordinaire. Thank you. Somehow you took this waterbed of words, picked it up, wrapped your arms around it, gave it structure, then set it back down without poking a hole in it. Your guidance throughout the editing process revealed a more polished manuscript that was buried somewhere between my psyche and psychosis.

To David Krull, from Krull Coaching. One does not endeavor on the journey of book writing successfully without others to push them forward when fear arises and pull them through when exhaustion overwhelms. Thank you for your support, encouragement, and accountability. Our ninety-day stretch goal turned into a two-and-a-half-year saga. I'll remember that the next time I agree to something of this magnitude! To Tyler Sit, for your friendship and guidance in all things social justice. Your feedback helped hone crucial sections of this book. To all the friends who helped with the comparative table. Thank you for your time, your comments, and your grace as I fumbled through a crash course in world religions. To everyone who donated to the GoFundMe campaign, particularly Jan and Iain Webber and Kim Peterson, your financial support helped make this book possible. To Greg Euclide for the custom cover art. I know of no better person, or artist, to convey the essence of soil and spirit through the universal language of visual medium. It is an honor to call you a friend. And finally, to Jeannie Larson, for being a mentor and friend in the world of all things nature. Though you may not remember, you helped this book germinate when you whispered the title in my ear so nonchalantly all those years ago.

Finally, I'd be remiss if I did not mention spiritual friends and mentors. To ye who shall not be named, thank you for teaching me to breathe in and breathe out. To the SoulForce team, for our exploration of all things BSC. Your friendship and acceptance make this path such a delight, and our experiences together helped shape every part of this text. Particularly, Kim Rose, for your energetic reading, revisions, and graphics for the book. To Lao Tzu, for writing a spiritual text that welcomed me "home" and continues to provide guidance for so many thousands of years later. To Sadhguru, for being a modern-day example of what's possible when clarity and consciousness align. And to all those who have come before me and are still to come after. To those who have come before, thank you for leaving a trail of breadcrumbs, signs, and guideposts along the path to awakening. For those who will come after, know that this book is not saying anything that hasn't already been said. Pick up your torch, and trust that your efforts will be rewarded as you journey from soil to spirit and back again. Remember, time is not as linear as many of us perceive, nor are dimensions as clearly defined as we might like to believe.

APPENDIX

Everyone has a different learning style, and I am not so igno-
rant as to think that this text will offer everything you need
or desire to awaken your life's core purpose. I have curated
a brief list of resources that may be helpful as you continue
your journey. I consider these people to have awakened their
life's core purpose. A brief synopsis provides a bit of context for each. Of course, you are encouraged to explore and
find your own resources that speak to you. When you find
them, please share with me at *ian@reviveuandi.com* or on
Instagram, Facebook, or Twitter, at *@reviveuandi.*

ECOLOGY & SPIRIT

Zach Bush
Resources: ZachBushMD YouTube channel and *The Rich
    Roll Podcast*

I have found no individual more capable of synthesizing the plight of human health and the profundity of human consciousness with exacting science. He is a thought leader in so many areas of the human experience and is truly architecting a healthier future for all of us. Look him up.

Robin Wall Kimmerer

Resources: Her 2013 book, *Braiding Sweetgrass,* and the *OnBeing* podcast

The Earth is in desperate need of individuals willing to cross the Rubicon and bridge the divide between industry, academia, and ecology. Robin Wall Kimmerer is the single most influential thought leader I know of illuminating the intelligence of plants and Indigenous wisdom.

Malidoma Patrice Somé

Resource: His 1994 book, *Of Water and the Spirit*

Malidoma Patrice Somé understands the connection between nature and intuition in a truly profound way. His unique background and upbringing, paired with his teaching, illustrate what is possible when a human is in touch with the true nature of their spirit.

HEALTH & WELLBEING

Brené Brown

Resources: Books, TED Talk, and podcasts

Simply put, Brené Brown is the bee's knees. Her research on courage, vulnerability, and leadership has gone viral for good reason. Not only is it a message the world needs to hear, but she is the perfect vessel to deliver it. Honest, open, authentic, and exceedingly funny, her content makes you enjoy the deep work of emotional vulnerability.

Pedram Shojai

Resources: The Urban Monk, both a book and a podcast

I have found no better resource for living a healthful life in the modern era. His book *The Urban Monk* is literally a field guide for designing a life conducive to health. His teachings lay an essential foundation that create physiological stability and a sound launching pad to pursue our highest calling. His writing reflects that of someone who has cultivated themselves deeply yet not lost touch with the world we live in.

CLARITY, PURPOSE, & VISION

Gary Keller & Jay Papasan

Resource: Their book, *The ONE Thing*

As far as I am concerned, there is no better resource for teaching one to eliminate the distractions in their life for the sake of awakening, or designing, their life's core purpose. Gary and Jay write with a clever, insightful, nuanced intelligence that does a better job of simplifying the unfathomable than any other book. There is a reason it is an international bestseller many times over. Do yourself a favor and pick up a copy.

SPIRITUAL LANDSCAPE

Sadhguru (Jaggi Vasudev)

Resources: His 2016 book, *Inner Engineering: A Yogi's Guide to Joy*, and his Sadhguru YouTube channel and podcasts

Sadhguru is a true gem amidst the sands of our collective awakening. His humor, insight, and spiritual teachings carve through the chaos of our time and distill thousands of years of ancient wisdom into actionable and inspirational guidance. He is a yogi, a mystic, a visionary, and so much more. Experience his wisdom for yourself if you have not already.

Hua-Ching Ni

Resource: His books *Workbook for Spiritual Development*
   and *The Complete Works of Lao Tzu*

Hua-Ching Ni is a prolific author. Having consumed many of his books, I would recommend beginning with the two listed above. There are many times in life where the desire for guidance or grounding emerges. Hua-Ching Ni provides both. His *Workbook for Spiritual Development* is well suited for someone already deep into the spiritual landscape of self-cultivation.

William Martin

Resource: His 2004 book, *A Path and a Practice: Using
   Lao Tzu's Tao Te Ching as a Guide to an Awakened
   Spiritual Life*

William Martin authored one of the most approachable translations of the *Tao Te Ching*, the most famous spiritual text from Taoist philosophy. His translation provides clear instruction for leading a spiritual life in the simplest of ways. I read a passage every morning, and each time I do, the text comes fully alive again and shows a new nature of its existence.

ADDITIONAL WRITINGS & TEACHINGS BY IAN C. WILLIAMS

AWAKEN Your Life's Core Purpose Guidebook

In Chinese martial arts, they bow with a right-handed fist, and a left-handed open palm. The right-handed fist represents attack, and the left-handed open palm represents self-discipline and restraint. The book in your hands is the open palm—useful theory and concepts, but sometimes lacking in direct application. The *AWAKEN Your Life's Core Purpose Guidebook* is the fist. It guides the user in self-reflecting applications intended to simplify the process of awakening your life's core purpose. If you are interested in diving deeper but unsure where to begin, or if you prefer a structured process to follow, consider it an additional resource on your journey.

To book Ian for a public speaking event, please visit *www.reviveuandi.com.*

To learn more about his consulting work, please visit *www.stillpointinsight.com.*

CPSIA information can be obtained
at www.ICGtesting.com
Printed in the USA
BVHW081549280223
659388BV00012B/639/J